mind.
body.
soul.

kendra leonard

BALBOA.PRESS
A DIVISION OF HAY HOUSE

This book is a work of non-fiction. Unless otherwise noted, the author and the publisher make no explicit guarantees as to the accuracy of the information contained in this book and in some cases, names of people and places have been altered to protect their privacy.

Balboa Press books may be ordered through booksellers or by contacting:

Balboa Press
A Division of Hay House
1663 Liberty Drive
Bloomington, IN 47403
www.balboapress.com
844-682-1282

Because of the dynamic nature of the Internet, any web addresses or links contained in this book may have changed since publication and may no longer be valid. The views expressed in this work are solely those of the author and do not necessarily reflect the views of the publisher, and the publisher hereby disclaims any responsibility for them.

The author of this book does not dispense medical advice or prescribe the use of any technique as a form of treatment for physical, emotional, or medical problems without the advice of a physician, either directly or indirectly. The intent of the author is only to offer information of a general nature to help you in your quest for emotional and spiritual well-being. In the event you use any of the information in this book for yourself, which is your constitutional right, the author and the publisher assume no responsibility for your actions.

Any people depicted in stock imagery provided by Getty Images are models, and such images are being used for illustrative purposes only. Certain stock imagery © Getty Images.

Print information available on the last page.

ISBN: 978-1-9822-4801-7 (sc)
ISBN: 978-1-9822-4800-0 (e)

Balboa Press rev. date: 11/19/2020

contents

the end

a week ago, i thought i was going to die. i had just received a massage, and had to be helped back to the locker room of the spa because i could barely walk. i was shaking with chills, so i decided to enter the steam room for some much needed heat. it became so overbearing that i left almost immediately and went into the sauna. then i realized, i needed to lay down. i was getting extremely light headed. shortly thereafter, i was asked if i was okay by someone who worked in the spa. i said yes, that i just needed a few minutes. but a few minutes later, i realized i was not okay. they got me some water and orange juice and asked if they should call someone. at first i said no, but then i noticed my hands were cramping shut like claws. i started to feel like something was very, very wrong. they told me they were calling the paramedics.

my partner in crime showed up along with my mother, watching me cramp and shake. afterwards they said it looked like i was having a seizure. the paramedics talked me into breathing back to normal as i begged for them not to let me die. i wondered if this was going to be it, or if my hands would be stuck in this shape forever. after they finally sat me up, i was dressed and taken out on the stretcher. when we got outside i felt like i was going to vomit, and i did, then they put me in the ambulance and took me to the hospital. they said i was extremely dehydrated and had a panic attack. i was not one to get panic attacks, as i usually thrive in stressful situations, but this time i thought for sure, that i was going to die.

after getting me to the hospital, i was put in a wheelchair in the waiting room. hours went by, they finally pulled me to the back, told me that i could either get an iv, or go home and drink a gallon of water. i opted for going home. no tests were run, and i was just happy to have made it this far and allowed to go home. my mother was the best caretaker ever, making sure i had everything i needed and wanted. i took a bath and went to sleep.

the next day, my entire body hurt all over. i just laid on the couch all day, watched all the harry potter movies with my mother. took a bath in the morning and another one at night, and i finally convinced her to go home and get some rest. the next morning i woke up at 3:45am. i felt good so i started to clean my place. next thing i knew, i was drenched in sweat. i took my temperature. it was at 101.7. then it dawned on me- maybe that's why i had sweat through my sheets. oh wait, maybe that's why i sweat through my sheets the night before. i decided to wait to go to urgent care instead of going to the emergency room.

when i got to urgent care, they tested me for the flu. based on all my symptoms, it made sense. however, i was not prepared for the diagnosis they gave me. i didn't have the flu, i had pneumonia. in fact, two of my upper lobes on my right lung were contaminated. they also told me that based on one of the tests that i might have a blood clot in my lung. i was like, 'pulmonary embolism?! i could die from that, right?!' i was shocked as i didn't have a cough or shortness of breath, and now they were telling me that i might have a life or death situation on my hands. they also informed me that this test could show a false positive, but the only way to know was to go back to the emergency room.

i arrived at the emergency room around 11:30am. they called me back a few hours later to run some more blood work. they set me up on an iv, i got some fluids and some antibiotics for the pneumonia, and then they took me to get a ct scan of my lungs. it showed that i did not have a blood clot, and they let me go home. still felt like complete shit, walking in slow motion, etc, but i was alive. the very next morning, i got a call from the hospital. they told me that my streptococcus pneumonia, which is the most common form of bacterial pneumonia, had gone into my bloodstream and i could become septic so i needed to come to the hospital asap for more antibiotics. i was like, 'sepsis?! i could die from that, right?!'

apparently they weren't that concerned cause even though i got there at 11:30am, they didn't call me back till 3:30pm for blood cultures. got sent out again till 5:30pm, when they finally brought me back for those good 'ol antibiotics. i was feeling the best i had felt in days, and since they didn't have a room available for me, i started doing yoga in the hallway.

just stretching, nothing crazy. finally, i looked at the doctor when they walked by and asked, 'so, 9:30, 10 o'clock, i can go home?' he said, 'you're not going anywhere. we are keeping you for at least a night, if not two.' they ended up keeping me for three. after the antibiotics and breathing treatment, my heart started to race. i asked the doctor to listen to my heart cause i thought it was going to pop out of my chest. he then mentioned that the breathing treatment can cause my heart rate to increase.

they gave me something to calm my heart down and at around 11:30pm, i was ready to fall asleep. they still didn't have a room ready for me, so i went to sleep in the hallway. at 3:30am (those seem to be my special hours), i was taken to the second floor. i had a roommate, which i felt awful disturbing her sleep, but every hour on the hour after that, i was interrupted by nurses checking on us both and getting vitals. i was so exhausted but, wait for it, 11:30am, i was finally given permission to not get vitals checked and get some rest. i fell asleep for a few hours, and woke up not feeling that great. fever was in and out, and more blood was drawn for more cultures. i was told i wasn't going anywhere.

the next day i felt good, but due to my fever, i had to stay another day. so i did a bunch of reading and relaxing, and hoped to not spike a fever. thankfully i slept through the night and the next morning i felt great. got up and took a shower and was told that i would be discharged in a few hours. that day there was a race in downtown. my street was blocked off, so my mother had to drop me off a block away from my place. i walked slowly towards my building and warned the cops blocking traffic that i had just been discharged from the hospital and to make sure i made it inside so my mother wouldn't have a heart attack.

my mom went to stock my fridge and pick up my meds, and when she came back i broke the news to her, she couldn't stay the night. i had made plans with a friend in my building for dinner, and i desperately wanted to be in my own space alone. i had just spent a week on and off in the hospital with my mother, and as much as i needed her then, i needed to be alone now. well, shortly after dinner was served, i started not feeling so great again. i had chills and when i got back to my place, i had a fever of 101.4. shit. i started a lukewarm bath, took some ibuprofen, and called the hospital. they said that if it didn't come down, i'd have to come back.

fortunately, it came down immediately and i slept the rest off. another day full of resting and restoring at home took place the next day, and when i invited my mother to join for dinner to calm her nerves, my fever spiked again, and she told me she was staying. had another day doing nothing and taking it easy. i made her leave this time. and finally, my fever left me for good. i finally felt like me again! well kinda me, but in slow motion. i couldn't take deep breaths and couldn't go anywhere or do anything, but i was finally on the mend. i called the hospital and asked if it was okay for me to take a little walk and go to a chill yoga class. they said i should be fine, just don't overdo it. so i took a little walk and went to a gentle yoga class that day, the next day, and the day after that.

by friday i was feeling like a new and improved me, so i took the opportunity to go visit my daughter in asheville. i met her at urgent care cause she had spiked a fever the last two days. she tested positive for the flu. fortunately her symptoms were gone and she was on the mend as well. we got to spend some much needed mother daughter time together over the weekend and i was so grateful to have the time with her. it was a good reminder of how amazing it is to have your mother take care of you when you're sick and how good it feels to take care of your daughter when she is not well. perspective- thank you mom…

you see, sometimes it takes things like this to knock you sideways where you have to depend on other people to take care of you. being a strong, independent woman, it is not easy for me to ask for help. that's when it takes someone who loves you so much to step in and do the things for you that you cannot ask for. and that's my mom. always there, always has been and always will be no matter what. even when you are at your wits end and snap at her for being there and being mom, she is still filled with love. and that's where i learned just how to love.

i love you, but i love me more

i have been searching for mind.body.soul. for several years now. my life had been so chaotic, that peace was the one thing that i wanted so very badly. being pregnant at twenty, widowed at thirty, opening a business, and everything in between, i had just been running nonstop. part of my roller coaster was the relationship that i was in. we were together for six years when i finally realized that i wanted to get married. you see, i never thought i wanted to get married. but we weren't moving forward, and relationships have to progress. it was after years of him kind of being non-committal, that my value, self esteem, and self worth were completely challenged. i became jealous and insecure. two traits that i did not like in myself. and that's what really was the trigger. i didn't like who i was becoming.

so much in love, but also a lot of pain. it was after several break ups and make ups that i realized something. as much as i loved this man, i loved me more. and i could no longer put myself through this. so i left the man that i wanted to spend the rest of my life with. it was one of the hardest things i had to do, and i've had to do a lot of hard shit in my life. but to come to the realization that i needed to love myself more than anyone else was a gift. and ultimately what i realized was that timing was everything. and it was time for us to come to an end. because this was the time for me.

i never really thought about it before, but i had never been alone. for nineteen years of my life i was in three serious relationships. i never knew i was a serial monogamist. i also realized i had a pattern when it came to men. i remember going to a therapist cause i thought i was sabotaging my relationship with my ex and after spilling my guts for an hour, she asked what my relationship was like with my father. i was like, 'i'm not talking about my father, i'm talking about my boyfriend.' then she said something so simple, yet so profound. 'you realize the first man you ever loved and were loved in return was your father and every future relationship with a man is based on that. same thing with your mother.'

whoa. mind blown. i never thought about that before. and yet, it made so much sense. you see, you take the good, bad, and the ugly from all those relationships and that's why they say 'you are a sum of your life's experiences.' think about it. they always say girls go for men who emulate their father. all the men in my life had anger issues, much like my father. i remember when i was very young, that all my father had to do was look at me, and i would burst into tears. for some reason, i subconsciously sought out this trait in the men i was with. talk about cycles and how history repeats itself. but how do we break the cycle?

i was told to rekindle the relationship that i had with my father and that would help my future relationships with men. i was told to write him a letter. after four months, i finally did. when i told my therapist, she asked if i gave it to him. i said, 'i thought you told me to write it for me.' she said, 'well, you wrote it, so you might as well give it to him.' i saw what she did there... and four months after that, i finally read it to him. before i did, i asked him if we could have some alone time. he questioned why, and i just told him i needed some time with just him. so when we were alone, i asked about his childhood.

as he explained things to me about his childhood, things really started to make more sense. you see, our personalities are formed by the age of five. and we tend to emulate the behavior shown by our parents. he definitely was becoming more like his father, and married my step-mother, who has similar qualities like his mother in some respects. we cried together and he told me i was right about everything. he only had one regret- not fighting for me and my sister- but he knew my mother would not stand for that, so he didn't even try. after our heavy conversation, we set a time to talk every week, very different from our current situation talking every several months for the past few years.

after a while, i asked my father to just call me whenever he felt like talking to me. i realized that he probably wanted to schedule a time to actually be able to speak with me because i am so busy, but i just wanted him to call me when he thought about me and wanted to speak with me. after that, we stopped talking regularly, and we went back to every so often. so, while i was recovering from pneumonia, i saw that he called me, but then he hung up as i went to answer the phone. i thought that maybe he called me by accident, but as i waited for him to call me back, he didn't. i got a little upset cause i had just gotten out of the hospital two weeks prior, and even if it was a butt dial, i would have thought that he would have at least checked on me to see how i was. nope.

the next day i spent with my mother and the following day i spent with my ex, now friends once again, so on the next day when i was talking to my daughter about the fact that i was upset, she said, 'just call him.' so i did. he answered with a 'what do you want' kinda thing, and i said, 'oh, i saw you called the other day, and normal kendra would have seen a missed call, but since i was in recovery mode, i saw you called, then hung up. i didn't know if it was a butt dial.' he said 'yes, it was an accident.' and then nothing.

so then he asked what i wanted. i kinda fumbled upon my words and asked how he was, my step-mom was, my step-sister. he then asked about my daughter. i told him that she was doing extraordinarily well in school, that she just found out that there was a sexual assault work crew that she could get on (part of a work-study program at her school) and since she wanted to do this for a living, what a great experience this would be. also mentioned that i couldn't remember if i had told him that she had been raped the summer before she went to school, so this would also be super helpful to her as well to get this training and experience to deal with her issues.

he then told me that his table was ready and maybe we could talk next week? like he didn't acknowledge anything, and no, he never called next week to follow up on that either. that was yet another time in my life that i realized the kind of relationship that i had with my father. my mother said 'he probably didn't hear you or wasn't even paying attention.' and i was like 'yea, that sucks too.' however, after speaking with my therapist about it, she mentioned that his reaction was not based in neglect, but that he just can't handle things emotionally, which also explains a lot of his anger. but that perspective explained so much, and i am grateful for it because it helped me understand that i was projecting my thoughts of how i thought he should have reacted instead of understanding where he was coming from and how that slight shift with context really helped it all make sense.

mercury in retrograde

other cycles that we continue to face are orbiting around the sun. for those of you who do not believe in the universe or astrology, i hope i can maybe shed some light that will help you understand. i, for one, have always been a firm believer in the zodiac. i am a true pisces- mutable, compassionate, contradictory, creative, emotional, gentle, intuitive, kind, nurturing, super spiritual, understanding, i could go on and on- and it's pretty solid every time i read up on my sign for the past 30 years. i'm pretty sure most of you do know that there are such things as stars and planets along with gravity and how they affect the universe, just like the moon affects the tide. so you have to consider then, that these things, do in fact, affect us as humans. i'm not an astrologer, but i cannot ignore the impact that these things have on our lives.

i'm not suggesting that one should alter their lives on what their horoscope says, but if you pay attention to it, it does lay out a foundational map to help you forecast or plan certain things in your life. ultimately we all have free will and the choice to do something or not do something, but according to the precise time and location of our birth, there is a chart that links you to the universe and your role in it. you see, we are all connected and all have purpose, some of us are just a little more tuned in than others. just like everything happening for a reason. and yes, there is a reason for everything. you may not know what it is and why it's happening, but i promise that in this wonderful world of chaos, too many 'coincidences' don't just 'happen.'

there is a reason you didn't get that job, get that green light, get that partner, get that opportunity. things always seem to fall into place and work themselves out, even when we are trying so desperately hard to make things go our way. and this is when mercury in retrograde seems to come into play. for those of you who don't believe or know what this means, i'm going to break it down for you like my spiritual guide broke it down to me. basically, imagine that we are going down the road at 70mph. well, when mercury goes retrograde, we are supposed to slow down to 55mph, but we end up pushing 80mph. this is when things go very wrong for us. and we wonder why shit is exploding in our face or things are not quite going our way.

mercury goes retrograde a few times throughout the year. mercury rules communication, technology, travel, and learning, so it is a good time to pause and reflect before making any big decisions concerning these areas. it's also not a good time to sign contracts, so you'll find it helpful to know when mercury is in retrograde depending on what you do. the reason people talk about mercury in retrograde is because it's a thing. just like every other cliche, the reason they exist is because they're true.

and yes, you can pick out certain things within the zodiac signs that sound like you just like people pick out what they do and don't like about religion, but overall, we have certain characteristics that do make up our signs. there is also compatibility within signs and one cannot ignore that some signs are just not meant to be together and some fit oh so very well. i highly suggest you take a look into your darkside zodiac as well. it's a humbling approach to all the not so nice things about your sign. but figuring out more about who you are and what makes you you, helps you be the best you. and who doesn't want to be the best version of themselves. i don't know about you, but i'm definitely in pursuit of what my purpose is in this life and how i can nurture it into fruition.

you talking to me?!

another thing that i think we need to pay attention to as a society, is how we speak to one another, treat one another. this is, yes of course, very obvious, but i'd like to take a minute to describe what is known as the japanese rice experiment by masaru emoto, japanese author and pseudoscientist who said that human consciousness has an affect on the molecular structure of water. okay, so here's what he did:

he took three jars of white rice and filled them each with water. every day, for thirty days he went to the first one and said, 'thank you,' went to the second one and said, 'you're an idiot,' and went to the third and completely ignored it. when i was told this story initially, i was told the sayings were 'i love you, i hate you, and ignoring you,' but you get the point. after a month, the one that was thanked fermented and gave off a pleasant aroma and was white on rice, the rice in the second beaker turned black and was all nasty, and the rice that was ignored began to rot, even worse off than the one that was hated.

according to scientists, water makes up 50-75% of the human body. this varies on whether you are a man, a woman, or a child. my interpretation of this experiment is that our words matter. our intentions matter. imagine if we constantly go around and say nice and thoughtful things to people. not only does it make us feel good to give love, but it feels good to receive it. for example 'i love you,' 'you are so beautiful,' 'i really appreciate you,' 'thank you for being you,' 'you are so wonderful,' etc. how does that even make you feel just reading those words? then imagine the opposite- 'you suck,' 'i hate you,' 'you're stupid,' 'you're ugly,' 'you're fat,' etc. these words do hurt. and lastly, imagine being ignored. is this what we do to people we feel uncomfortable with, outcasts, homeless, the disabled, the elderly? how do you think they feel inside?

the point is, we can change not only ourselves, but other people simply by the way we speak to them, or simply acknowledging their presence as a human being on this earth. we are internalizing all of the things that we are saying to ourselves as we look in the mirror every morning (i'm fat, i'm ugly, no one likes me) and we are making it come true. when we say those things to ourselves, or allow others to say them to us, we become that way. when we begin to love on ourselves and speak to ourselves with love, we can turn that outward to the world at large and love on them as well. simply complimenting someone on their outfit, or laughing at someone's joke, even smiling at someone as you pass by them on the sidewalk, all of these simple gestures can transform someone's day.

but this transformation must take place from within. love yourself and you'll see just how much better you feel. you wouldn't allow someone to talk to you or treat you with disdain, so why do we accept it from ourselves? we shouldn't, and that's the starting point. people who are happy show it. it's hard to ignore. their happiness is contagious and these are the people you want to be around. people who are consumed with hating on themselves and others, well, that shows too. they are sucking the life out of themselves and others. they are the ones who you feel depleted by in their presence. you just had the energy sucked out of you. there is a reason that misery loves company. and for those who are just completely disregarded and ignored, just how hollow or empty they are on the inside? they are basically dying from the inside out. we are all connected and need to be in order to survive in this world. through human connection and nature we grow abundantly. without it, we shrivel up and live a meaningless existence.

our entire society is heading in this direction. although i do feel like there is a movement going on, and i am definitely on the bandwagon trying to save the universe, we need more people to become aware. most people walk down the street with their head down, or looking at their phone. people don't even know how to function without their phone. we have become so disconnected as a society, some people don't even know how to have a conversation, how to make eye contact, how to be genuine and sincere. it is so sad. there is this false reality on social media where people use it as a platform to hide in plain sight. sure they post all the time and look perfect, but how do they feel?!

kendra leonard

maybe it's just me, but i feel like technology has robbed us of our soul. i had a doctor interview me not too long ago on how technology could help the retail world. i sat and thought about this for a minute and finally said, 'i would love technology to help reconnect us as humans by removing technology from our daily lives.' we have become a victim to our phones and social media, and it really is taking our time away from us, and time is running out. being present and in the moment and full of love could do us all a little bit of good.

you are what you eat...

so a few years ago, my boyfriend at the time was a vegetarian. therefore i decided to try and be a vegetarian too (it's a pisces thing, you know, picking up on the traits of our partners). every time we would break up, i would have an 'i eat meat' party, you know, just to spite him, in spite of myself of course. anyway, even though we were together for years and i would always go back to being a vegetarian when i was with him, it wasn't enough for him. he wanted me to be a vegetarian for the right reasons, which i admire, but i was always just a suppressed meat eater. anyway, one year for christmas he bought me this book, *eating animals* by jonathan safran foer. this guy wasn't a vegetarian either, but he did look into the moral reasons behind vegetarianism, the farming industry, and the food that we choose to eat everyday.

imagine that you are a chicken. your life span is 37 days. during those 37 days, you are in a 12x12 cage, stacked 12x12, pissing and shitting on your friends, not able to go outside and play, no peace, no quiet, no fun. kind of depressing. now imagine you're a pig. you're hanging out with all your friends, rolling around in the mud. then, all of the sudden, you go missing behind a trap door. all your friends are like, 'whoa! where did they go? omg, do you remember when so and so disappeared that day and they were never seen again?!' meanwhile you're like, 'what the fuck is going on and where am i?' you are anxious and scared and thinking the worst. now imagine that you are a cow. you're hanging out in the meadow eating grass and soaking up the rays of sunshine until your master takes you on a short walk down a dark hallway where something knocks you on the head that should have rendered you unconscious. but it doesn't. and you are now being skinned alive.

sorry for the imagery here, but these are all things that happen in the farming industry. sure we don't like to think about them, but this is kind of the fucked up way that we enjoy fried chicken, bacon, and burgers. and the most alarming thing second to these animals living a horrible existence and being slaughtered for our benefit, is the fact that they are depressed, anxious, scared, confused, etc. and we are ingesting all of that. think about it. is one of the reasons we are so depressed, anxious, fearful as a society because we are eating animals that had those same feelings? hunters who don't kill their prey immediately do not eat the meat because it has turned. imagine being a deer and getting shot but not killed. you are going to be freaking out and that has to do something to you internally.

now i have been questioned about this by a person or two who says that animals don't have feelings. anthropomorphism is the attribution of human traits, emotions, or intentions to non-human entities. it is considered to be an innate tendency of human emotion. however, and i don't have pets, but i bet any of my friends who have dogs or cats or any other animal would attest to their pets having a personality and feelings. and some have even said, they don't feel pain. i'm pretty sure that every time a paw is stepped on or tail is closed in a door, there is a painful reaction verbally and instinctively by whatever animal is being harmed. this leads me to another outrageous travesty that occurs in our culture.

circumcision

recently, it had been brought to my attention that years ago, doctors thought that male babies couldn't feel pain and therefore were not given any anesthesia prior to being circumcised. don't believe the hype. again, i'm pretty sure if you ask any parent listening to their baby cry, they can tell you which wail is the painful one. anyway, let me start at the beginning of when this came up. (all puns intended, always). not too long ago i met a guy who decided as an adult to get circumcised. he followed what his urologist said and didn't do enough due diligence and even though his doctor swore he wouldn't feel any difference having sex, he did. it all changed. he would never again have what he once experienced. now, this was a decision that he made as an adult.

but most men don't have the choice. their parents make it for them. and most of their parents, just go through the motions. hmmm, a common theme in life, yes? some parents that i've spoken to don't even remember being asked if they wanted their son circumcised. it has become the norm of our society to mutilate baby boys within the first two days of birth and no one is talking about it. we talk about female mutilation all the time and how horrific it is (and it is) in other cultures. and how could they do that??? savages. of course, i agree, but it also begs me to ask the question, why are we doing that??? are we savages too?

well, after i watched *american circumcision* on netflix in addition to talking to a bunch of other people about it, i was blown away. so this documentary starts off with this cute little baby boy being taken from his hospital bed, wheeled down a hallway, looking at the lights passing by, being brought into this room where a tiny plastic bed with arm and leg restraints are awaiting him. he is tied down, cleaned, given some anesthetic, his foreskin is separated from the head of the penis by a special instrument called a probe, next a bell shaped device is fitted over the head of the penis and under the foreskin. the foreskin is then pulled up and over the bell and a clamp is tightened around it to reduce the blood flow to the area and a scalpel is used to cut and remove the foreskin.

and that's it! that's how it is most commonly done. i won't take you through the other two methods as i feel like this may be enough for you to handle in a day. and this has been going on since the beginning of time. this 'practice' was adopted by jewish people as a religious ritual, then the christians continued the practice. one way they explained this 'acceptable' form of male mutilation, was it 'purified' them and society by reducing sexuality and sexual pleasure because it was seen as 'dirty' or 'impure.' it is known that the male foreskin is THE principal location of erogenous sensation and by removing it, reduces that same sensation.

now that you're done swallowing that, are you not about to hop on this bandwagon to make sure we never mutilate another male ever again?! now, there are arguments that it is 'unclean' to not be circumcised. well, aren't we taught how to clean ourselves? don't we get told to clean behind our ears, in between our toes, in all of our crevices? shouldn't foreskin be the same thing?

so no, there is no medical reason to clip the tip of a penis off. also, if you are a christian, don't you believe in god and that he designed us in all of his glory? do you think he made a mistake and forgot to take the tip off so we therefore had to refine his work? i don't think so...

oh, and let me mention here that america is the only country that widely practices mutilating their boys. is that to make it easier on parents to not have to teach them how to clean another body part? is that because sex is dirty? another taboo that we americans can't seem to discuss like death? we are the only country that seems to do things without questioning the source. we literally are like cattle being herded. we don't know where we're going, we just follow where everyone else is going/doing. we don't question people whose words don't match up with their actions and call them on it. we don't want to do anything that rocks the boat or makes anyone feel uncomfortable. oh, but we'll cut the tip off of every penis being born in the country, no problem.

the male penis was designed with a foreskin for many reasons. first, it's meant to protect it. as it is flopping around in the wind, in between the legs, it could get hurt. the foreskin is the first line of defense. second, and possibly the most important, the foreskin has a ton of nerve endings to stimulate the penis. hello, pleasure! why are we trying to take away pleasure from men? is this why many of them, are not satisfied, thrusting harder and harder to try to feel something, have violent tendencies, have allowed the porn industry to go out of control?

this was the first interaction they had with their penis. again, from a predominately white american background, which is also where the serial killers are from i might add, don't we think that pain went somewhere? from the moment boys are running around and they fall, they are told to 'act like a man, don't cry.' why are we making our young male children so hard? is this why some are emotionally inept? is this why they can't communicate their feelings properly and have to punch something? is this why sports is such a widely acceptable form of conversation and way of life? aggression, anger, comparing penises, the list goes on.

however, what can happen to these males not only alters their lives sexually, but physically. there are such things as botched penises. are they hung to the left or to the right? down or up? does it hurt for them to have an erection? botched jobs have been known to happen and now when all we were doing was trying to make all the little penises look the same cause we can't be different in american society, we now have deformed or malformed penises. i know a lot of people say that they don't want the child and the father to look different, but again, can't we have a conversation to explain that 'honey, daddy's parents didn't know that there wasn't a medical reason to not perform this procedure. they just did what everyone was doing back then. now, we know better, and we don't want to alter your body or cause you physical harm, let alone take any pleasure away from you.' why is that so damn hard? (just wait till i start writing children's books).

sadly, for many reasons, it seems like the number one reason we do this is for aesthetic! maybe for those of you who don't know, once you pull down the foreskin, it looks the same. but did you see what you read? people mutilate their boys because they don't like the way it looks. wow. so, if i don't like my baby's brown eyes, should i change them? why is it acceptable for us to alter the physical appearance of another human? so we all look the same?? obviously, i thought about this a lot and asked several men, and women for that matter, about it.

the men did say that growing up in the locker room was a thing and a few that were not circumcised did feel judged and got picked on in school. cause some kids are assholes. but as adults, are totally fine with it, especially knowing that they have the upper hand when it comes to sexual pleasure. oh, and lasting longer than five minutes. again, imagine you have this overwhelming feeling inside you your entire life and you just can't seem to even fill this void (of your clipped dick) and you finally get a taste or touch of it and oops. sorry. it makes sense. you guys just need to enjoy a lot more foreplay and know that it gets better the longer you take.

the ladies had a mixture of remarks. apparently they like the way they looked without the foreskin cause that's what they were used to (or had ever seen). but the ones who had been with both, didn't have any complaints. but you don't know what you don't have or haven't had. unfortunately, for the majority of american men, they will never know what they are missing and what pleasure they could have had sexually that was taken from them moments after they were born. sadly, this one can't be reversed…

i'm single, now what..?

when i had been single for about a year, i finally broke down and got on tinder. not something i wanted to ever do as i would much rather meet someone organically then online, but hey. i was in mexico. but i'm not going to tell you that story. that was international tinder. only a few people get that one out of me. no, i was in atlanta. cause there was no way in hell i was going to do tinder in raleigh. too many people knew me. so i chatted with a few, but there was no way i was going to leave my ladies to go meet up with someone, so that was it. though i did meet a gentleman who was married but in an open relationship. i had only one other person in my life who exposed me to this world and i was intrigued.

not intrigued cause i wanted to be involved, but had never heard of this type of relationship and therefore could not wrap my brain around it. like most critics, when presented with something new and out of the norm, you question it, judge it, are repulsed by it., etc. then, when you listen and get information, your mind can be opened. well, i was interested, but still not going there. the man that i had met continued texting me after i had left atlanta and we developed a friendship. he was somewhat of a shaman and basically told me my life story up until this point. that i have been giving and giving and giving so much of myself to so many people all my life and now it was my turn to receive. i could totally get down with that.

i couldn't help but feel guilty for speaking with him, even though he told me he was in an open marriage, and then he said his wife wanted to speak with me. we chatted for a bit, and i still felt a little awkward, and shortly thereafter, our conversations ceased. oh, and of course i had turned off tinder the moment the flight landed in raleigh, so there's that. but one night, i was encouraged to get back on and start swiping. matched with a gentleman who ended up asking me out for a drink. it was a thursday night and we met at a bar. i almost didn't want to go, but i'm a woman of my word so i showed up. after our first drink and a great start, he admitted the same thing, but was glad he came. he then asked if i wanted another cocktail.

we enjoyed our second drink over good conversation, and after we were done he asked if i had plans or if i was free. i told him my only plans were hanging out with him, but i was hungry and a girl needed to eat. i told him he didn't have to pay for anything but i was going to sitti to get a filet. (the frequent place of my break up and eat meat experience). we had a nice dinner and a bottle of wine, then he was like, 'so you want to continue?' i said, 'sure!' and we moved on to another spot. we got another drink and he asked if i had any vices. i told him sometimes when i drink, i like to smoke. so we went outside to smoke a cigarette. then pearl jam's *black* came on, and i said 'aw, this is one of my favorite songs,' and he was like, 'who are you?!'

i told him i owned a store down the street and we should totally go there and open up a bottle of wine and i could read him his darkside zodiac (also really fun to do with someone you just met). we went inside and i turned off the lights (we always keep them on for people to see inside at night) and put on portishead radio. rearranged some furniture so we could sit and read and opened a bottle of wine. i read and we laughed and after i was done, we went outside for another cigarette. we went back in and he read me mine. more good times, but this time he went to the bathroom, and i went outside to smoke a cigarette. as i was about to light up, two guys walked by offered to light it for me, as gentlemen should do. well, one of them accidentally hit my wine glass and all of my red wine went pouring down my dress. but, my dress was made of neoprene, so it rolled off of me like a superhero. the guys were dumbfounded.

about this time, my date walked out of the store to find us laughing on the sidewalk. we all chatted for a bit and then i invited them in so that i could read them their darkside zodiac. we laughed, we talked, drank more wine, then the next thing i remember was waking up to a phone call. it was 10:15am, mind you i should have opened my store at 10am. it was a gentleman that i helped the day before. so i got up, took care of him, checked the perimeter, and made my way back to my oversized chair that i had been sleeping in. the doors were locked and the premises along with myself were secure, so i took in the scene.

four wine glasses, four bottles, candle wax all over the floor next to the *darkside zodiac* by stella hyde and lantern light were all around me. what a night. at 10:30am, i got another phone call from a guy i helped the day before and got up to take care of him. afterwards i still went back to the chair. at 10:45am i got another phone call. it was a guy who said he hung out with me at my store the night before and he tracked his phone there. yep! i was sitting on it. it was at this point that i decided i needed to get up and open my store. i went to the bathroom, brushed my teeth and as i was leaving the bathroom, my cohort walks in and says 'what is gong on?, i've been texting you all morning. wait, you had that on yesterday.' i confessed my sins and told her that it was not okay that i did it, but definitely not okay if she ever did.

thank goodness i own a clothing store so i could change my clothes. obviously the details were a little fuzzy, so she just said, 'ask your tinder date.' so i reached out and said, 'so, you left?' he responded with 'well, when you came out of the stockroom with the other guy, i didn't feel like i should stick around.' my mouth dropped to the floor. no way i would have done that. i said, 'no way, i would never do anything like that.' he said, 'yea, it was kind of awkward for me and his friend.' i was like, 'oh shit. i'm so sorry.' he said, 'it's okay, you don't owe me anything, we were just having a great time, it sucks it ended like this.' it was at this moment that it dawned on me that i had invited two guys in on our date…

it was also about this time that i kinda forgot (due to my unforeseen series of events from the night before) that i was having lunch with a friend from out of town. we had been friends for about 20 years and worked at banana republic together. he was now a traveling shaman of sorts. he was auditing doctorate level courses, teaching yoga and mindfulness, carrying around all of his 40 articles of clothing and essentially homeless by choice, but traveling the world, living a full life, traveling from one monastery to the next. it was this man that calmed my madness for the moment who was so peaceful and listening to all that had transpired in my life in the last several years that we had seen each other, that i couldn't help but feel his energy overwhelm me. he spoke with intention and grace and love and we picked up just where we had left off a few years ago. he seemed all the more wise and shared his light and experience with me as we sat having lunch.

our time passed within moments, but was full enough to slow down time for a while, and then it was back off to work for me. i had to make a run to the bank, but didn't want to miss the opportunity to speak with the guy who was coming to pick up his phone from the night before. so i told my partner in crime to not let him leave if he came when i was gone. of course, i was still a little hazy on all the events that had happened the previous night, so once again, she suggested i ask my tinder date for more details. so naturally i reached out once again to get the blanks filled in. i asked, 'would you mind shedding some light as to what occurred last night, cause obviously i can't remember.' to which he replied, 'with all due respect kendra, you want me to give you the details of how you made out with another man when you were on a date with me?' my response, 'ouch.' he since blocked me.

it was right about this time that i got informed that the man from the night before came to get his phone. when i approached him, i said, 'so, what exactly happened last night?' he said, 'i'll text you.' he finally did and basically said something like, 'all i remember is making out with a beautiful woman, namely you, for hours. when i left, the sun was coming up and the birds were chirping.' and when he said that, all the dots connected in my brain, and the memory of all of these things came rushing back to the surface. that is exactly what happened. and now it was confirmed, single kendra is dangerous…

the vortex

so that little experience led into my weekend, where the continuation of being single and spending time with my ladies that night for an engaging dinner followed by drinks and dancing for that friday and saturday. on sunday, i had to work. at the time, i was not regularly working sundays. and normally i don't drive to work either, but on this one fine sunday i did because i needed to flee quickly to yoga to get in a workout before meeting my friend from overseas. another friend whom i had known for 20 years. when i opened my car door to cross the street, it immediately started down pouring. i thought to myself, 'well, this day is gonna suck.' (no one shops when it's raining).

but, upon entering my store, i chatted with my intern before he left, and was helping a mother daughter duo who hadn't been into the new location yet. and they were, wait for it, shopping!! (people like to look around a lot, but people don't always take the time to actually shop and try on clothes anymore- makes me sad). anyway, in this happiest of moments, another client came in who had been in yesterday with her boyfriend for the first time in the new location, came back alone to do more shopping. i was ecstatic! thinking that it would be a very quiet day with little to no clients and here were three women (which by the way, aren't shopping as often as men are these days) who were letting me help them try on clothing and having a blast doing it.

as i finished up with the mother daughter duo, the other client from the day before was trying on clothing in the fitting room. she had only been in my previous store once and we had a moment and cried together (which i do often with clients) and she bought my first book. she and i were talking through the curtain (which i love to do) about life and such and somehow i mentioned my lifepath number. she asked what mine was and when i told her i was an 8, she said, 'i can totally see that.' i asked what that meant cause although i had recently figured out what my life path number was, i never looked to see what it meant. she told me to go look it up.

i was blown away. like wow. (you should all go add up each individual number of your birthday and find out what your life path number is right now- also fun to do with people you've just met). anyway, after that, my day just kept getting better. from that client on, every person who walked into my store was a new client. and they all were drinking the koolaid! energy flowing between me and each one of them was magical and uplifting. of course i was brought to tears several times, followed by extreme happiness, but all of the sudden, this overwhelming feeling kept getting bigger and bigger. with each new interaction, my heart levels were being filled. almost to the point of explosion.

that was the only way i could describe it. and i'm a woman of a million words. literally i kept saying, 'i can't, i can't, i can't, i can't, i can't' cause i couldn't come up with words to describe this overwhelming feeling of love and joy. the way that i finally did describe this to people was that my heart was so abundantly full of love that if a feather just lightly touched my heart it would explode into a million magic fairy dust particles all over raleigh. my daughter called during this experience and asked if i was tripping on acid cause i sounded crazy. (disclosure- i wasn't and didn't have anything else in my system either).

it was also around this same time that my friend from banana republic asked if he could come by the shop and hang for a bit. upon his arrival, i asked if he was doing this or had anything to do with this feeling i had. he said that this was all the love that i have poured out to the universe over my lifetime and it was now being brought back to me. it was all my doing. i was floating. he spent the rest of the afternoon with me, maybe an hour or so, and instead of rushing off to go to yoga, he suggested that we meditate in the park. i didn't know what that meant. i had never meditated before. so he led me through a breathing exercise, a body exercise, and a light exercise.

i felt like i was breathing for the first time. even though i had been taking yoga for a year or two and had always been trying to 'find my center' i had never really succeeded. so for the first time, i was really breathing. feeling my breath enter into my nostrils, hit the back of my throat, go down my trachea and into my lungs where they filled up with oxygen. over and over. felt my chest rise and fall. i also felt my blood flowing through my veins for the first time- literally the heat, the flow. then lastly, he talked me through a light exercise. imagining this ball of light coming from within my body and almost 'turning everything on' and finally it escaped me and went out into the universe in the massive, expansive light covering everything.

now i know it may sound like i was on something, but really, i was just high on life. when i opened my eyes, i felt like i was seeing for the first time. the leaves on the trees were so green, and the sky, it was the bluest blue i had ever seen. and the air touching my skin was almost caressing it in a way. my senses were heightened and i was in complete awe. i shared my experiences with him and he said something very simple to me. he said, 'kendra, all of these things have been here, just as they always have been. the only thing that has changed is you. you have just now become aware.' he also explained that this feeling would not last forever and that i needed to learn how to channel it and ask the universe for more. this was the vortex. it was at this time that my other friend traveling from across the globe texted me and told me he was already at my place.

now i had to move, but felt like my little baby ankles made of delicate bone that might shatter like an eggshell and crumble beneath me, but my shamanic friend explained that i just needed to take one step at a time. i felt like i was an infant learning how to walk for the first time. i was feeling all of my toes, and the bottom of my feet, and my heels, and my ankles, and my legs, and my arms for the first time again. then i had to drive. you get my point. everything was brand spankin' new. i gave love to my friend and thanked him for enlightening me and tried to presently rush (while enjoying/embracing every moment) in my car to my other friend who was patiently waiting for me to learn how to walk again.

when i got to my place five minutes later, i was still in the overjoyed feeling of calmness and tried to explain the situation to my friend that had been waiting. i was grateful that he had known me for 20 years or so cause i know i sounded like a lunatic. we were walking to a bar to watch *game of thrones* and on the way, ran into some people that i knew. i hugged them and told them a brief synopsis (if that's even possible) of my journey on this day and they, too, looked at me like i was kinda crazy. by the time we got to our destination, i had finished giving my friend all the details of the day and got that out of my system. or so i thought.

i ran into several other people that i knew and tried to explain this overwhelming feeling of my heart being so full, but i was told to go get a drink, etc. i knew i sounded a bit much, but i couldn't contain myself. i think the only way i was really ever to calm down was that i had to shut the fuck up for an hour to watch *game of thrones*. it took all of my composure to sit there quietly, but i managed. *game of thrones* has a good way of doing that to you. afterwards my friend and a friend of a friend from germany started conversing in german and everything was sympatico. i wondered, 'is this what peace feels like?'

at some point in the conversation, i figured out everyone's life path number and shared the good info. we talked into the night and the next morning was 7.17.17 (that number is the same forwards and backwards, by the way. plus my favorite number in life has always been 7 or 17, and my life path number was 8. numerology is a thing ladies and gents. anyway…)

the next day, my daughter and i were headed for london. she told me not to talk to anyone at the airport cause i sounded crazy still and she was worried they wouldn't let me on the plane. fortunately i was able to contain myself mostly and we made it to london. another great story, but that one will have to wait…

the path to enlightenment

from that time on, i felt like it was my duty to inform people of their life path number. also, hugs. did you know that you need four hugs a day to survive? eight hugs a day to maintain? and twelve hugs a day to grow? are you thriving or are you barely surviving?! once i was charged with this knowledge i was hugging everybody all the time. not that this wasn't in my normal nature, but i was taking this to a whole new level. years ago in college when i was taking my psychology class, i remember hearing about an experiment that was done in the 40's in an orphanage where the babies were fed, bathed, changed, and had all of their basic needs met, but zero love and affection or even words were spoken to or eye contact with their care providers. all of them died. all of them.

this is not only a very disturbing experiment, but also should be a wake up call to every human on this earth. we, as humans, are meant to be loved. we are meant to be touched, and hugged. this is how empathy is formed at the early stages of life and this is how we are all meant to survive- and thrive- in love! over the course of the last few years in my hug research with individuals that i met, it was alarming to me just how many people didn't think they even got four hugs a week! how sad! no wonder we are so lost, sad, depressed, alone, anxious, etc. we aren't getting enough love! for those of you not getting enough love in your life, make a commitment today to start seeking out 12 hugs a day. i bet your life would completely transform. not to mention the lives of others. try it...

so on my journey of hugging the nation, i realized over time that i was starting to deplete my own energy source. i started being a little more selective of who i hugged. it didn't dawn on me that by giving so much love out, that i forgot i needed to love on myself in solitude a little more. it takes lots of energy to save the universe. anyway, one of the ways of loving on myself was by going to hot yoga. it was around this time that i was going to 11 classes a week. those were my peak weeks. worst case scenario, 4 classes, on average, 7. and of course i thought that this was one of the best ways to give back to myself. physical activity, being centered, resting and reflecting.

i had been into my practice for a few years at this point and one day, after class, i decided to try a headstand. not something i was really working on hard core, but wanted to give it a go. and finally, for the first time, i felt like i had achieved it. i was light as a feather, i was floating, it was one of the most amazing feelings i had felt. but then something happened. i got out of the feeling and started thinking. i started to fall backwards, and my neck went crunch, crunch, crack. i was like fuck, fuck, fuck. i laid there for a minute and someone grabbed me some ice. i got up and knew something was wrong. obviously the pain and after going to the chiropractor, it was discovered that i tore three ligaments in my neck.

and that was the beginning of my relationship with my chiropractor. i have been going for almost three years now to see him every three weeks or so. it is amazing to me how incredibly everything is linked in your life as it pertains to your body and mind. there is a wisdom that all of us possess in our very own precious system and being in tune and tuned-up is critical for our success. so i added this treatment to my monthly routine. it's just like getting a haircut. your body needs love too.

through all of this love that i have been giving and receiving over the last several years, i've realized that the most important person you can love is yourself. hopefully by getting to know myself better, i will honor myself and know my self worth. no one is going to love us like we love ourselves. and that is just what i decided to do. i made the decision that i was going to do whatever the fuck i wanted to do, whenever the fuck i wanted to. i started making dates with myself. i found it very hard to commit to anyone else during this time. because i am a woman of my word, if i said i was going to do something, i was going to do it. so i just left it open. 'maybe,' i'll let you know,' 'we shall see' were common phrases that i would use when i wasn't sure how i would feel so i could be true to myself.

i also started walking a lot. with no real direction or intention of where i was going or what i was doing. it was just simply enjoyable to see where the earth took me. sometimes it took me hours of just walking around thinking, other times it crossed my path with friends or strangers and great conversations. and being that i was alone, i could also excuse myself from the situation when i felt like i needed to be alone again or needed to move on. being alone helped me listen to myself and what i wanted. it was the first time in my life that i was taking care of me. another new thing for me. putting myself first for once. and it felt great. i was truly investing in myself. and when you pour all this love into yourself, you attract the love you so desire and deserve.

obviously i wasn't ready to do this until now. i needed to go through all of the things that led up to this point, to get to this realization- timing is everything. when i think of all my relationships and when we met and how things evolved and how things fell apart, they all had divine timing.

gift from the gods

so it was time to go to market. it was a whirlwind of a wonderful time and in the morning of the last day, i got a text from a rep that we had met last february at the tradeshow in chicago. the day before we met, my partner in crime and i had been walking our usual fast walk through the aisles and a woman approaching us had on black patent leather pants. well, this only matters cause my cohort was wearing over the knee high patent leather boots. of course, as they approached each other, they smiled and strutted in their matching patent leather and took a photo and we all moved on.

the next day, the guy that shared the booth with the woman who posed for a pic told her to invite us in. she did and immediately i was overwhelmed by the amount of incredibly interesting patterns on shirts that i had ever seen. this was strange because i was not really drawn to patterns. my partner in crime said it was weird too. the gentleman explained that the designer had gone to MIT and each pattern had an algorithm. he also told me they had ties and cuff links. when i gazed upon the cufflinks, it all hit me. the cufflinks were gears of a watch. my late husband loved timepieces. we had 37 clocks in our house. (the only reason i know that piece of information is when my daughter in 2nd grade had to count things in our home- tables, chairs, clocks, etc. and daylight savings time sucks). the reason i was so attracted to this brand is cause it reminded me of him.

i had a moment, cried, and returned to shopping. we placed an order and we went on our merry way after we had a lovely interaction with these two new beautiful souls. well, back to the original story. it was now august and we were in vegas. that rep asked us where we were, that we were his favorite- i said we were on our way today. when we got to the booth, we hugged him and started talking. but then there was this voice behind me asking 'just how single are you?' i turned around to this absolutely gorgeous man and responded, 'i'm 100% single, and i'll take you and your brother.'

he was half lebanese, half french, tall, dark, handsome, and had the most amazing eyes, smile, and dimples. he asked if he could embrace me. i said 'absolutely.' we got to talking about him and his brand and mine, and he said, 'omg. you're the one. the one with the book. the one who lost your husband to cancer.' i affirmed all of that and he showed me a pic on his phone of a white shirt that had little red and black what looked like lines from a distance, to saying 'f#ckcancer' and 'we're going to beat it.' they too had raised money for cancer research- over 1 million. he asked to hug me again. of course, i obliged. oh, and did i mention he could dress?! he was also a scorpio whose birthday just happened to be a day after my late husband and the meaning of his middle name, also the name of his brand, was the title of this chapter.

after we placed the order, he asked me to dinner. i told him that we already had plans with another rep and i was a woman of my word and could not break plans. he said he respected that more than i'll know, and then asked for my phone and proceeded to put his number and saved it as the 'love of my life.' well i was smitten. anyway, he said we would find a way to connect somehow. he also said he knew that i had a lot of work to do, but he wanted me to come back and hug him -like every thirty minutes. i was like, yea, no, but as we walked by on our way down the opposite direction i did sneak through to give him a kiss on the neck. on the way out, we met two of his clients that he had known for years in which the wife of the gentleman she was with said, 'not only is he beautiful on the outside, he has a heart of gold.' i had everything i needed to know.

upon arriving at our next appointment with our rep that we had a dinner date with, he informed me that we actually never solidified plans and i should definitely go out with the guy that was making me glow. so i immediately texted him and let him know that i was officially free for dinner. i was so excited. i don't normally get excited about men very often. i got ready quickly after the show and i took an uber so i wouldn't be late (i'm a pisces, i'm always late. or as i like to say now, 'i arrive precisely at the right moment.') well my uber driver picked me up and made a u-turn and we were there. he literally lived right next to our hotel.

he came to get me and told me that even though he wanted to take me on a romantic date for two, all of his people said no, that he couldn't have me to himself, so they were coming and i was about to meet his mother. she was visiting and he had already told her all about about me, that he doesn't normally introduce people to his mother, but i was special and here we went. so i walked in and met some of his friends and accounts and then his mother. we walked arm in arm and he asked what i wanted to do for my birthday. i mentioned tokyo and he said 'let's do that.' i then adjusted it to italy, my all time favorite country.

we arrived in front of the restaurant- cpk. i have to admit i was a little disappointed. all these amazing restaurants in vegas and this is where we're going? but i'm a food snob. fortunately, none of that mattered, cause he ordered food for the table of ten and the whole time it was like it was just us two. he told me his life story. and couldn't believe he was disclosing this information to me. apparently he was telling me things that no one knew about him. (i tend to have that effect on people). we left the restaurant and then i found myself playing cornhole- again, not my speed. so here i am, in my favorite outfit in heels playing this. i sucked at it, but enjoyed myself. then we made our way back to his place.

i was feeling sickness in my throat before dinner began, so i got some emergen-c on the way back. i was downing them like crazy when his brother warned that the vitamin c would keep me up all night, but i ignored and kept drinking. as i did, we spoke about business and such. one by one, people disappeared to go to sleep, until is was just three, so finally, i said 'i guess i should go.' he walked me downstairs and outside and that's when he grabbed my face and started kissing me. holy shit. well that happened over the next several minutes and as we were inspiring love making on the streets of vegas, we paused, then went inside to the lobby. he said he wished he could invite me up or to his other place, but i told him i'm obviously not going to be making out with him next to his mother.

we decided the lobby wasn't as comfortable as outside, so we went back outside. after several more minutes of embracing each other and finding our way around each other, he eventually started pushing me away and told me to leave. i explained that i wasn't done with him just yet. so then i invited him back to my place. he said if he came back he'd probably rape me. i told him that i didn't know if that was a cultural difference or language barrier, but he couldn't say things like that. not that i would let him. i wasn't inviting him back to have sex, but we could do other things that we couldn't on the street. he said no, that i should go, and told me he wanted me for the long term, not just one night. years later, today in fact, we still communicate and the long distance love affair still lingers.

female revolution

on this note, i feel like it is pertinent to mention that it is time to discuss sexual freedom. as a woman, it has long since been deemed that if she has sex with more than one person, that she is a slut. i would beg to differ. though i had only been with three men for the majority of my life, each six to seven years, not only did i realize that i was a serial monogamist, but that i really enjoyed having sex. and just cause i was single, didn't mean that i wasn't going to have any either. of course i have to have a connection with someone, but i also act like a little girl when approaching the physical act of being with someone. i definitely require the man to make the first move.

so again the thought, just cause i'm single doesn't mean that i'm not going to have sex. and then i thought, oh, is this what 'friends with benefits is all about?' i mean, i'm attracted to men, and when having a meaningful conversation and chemistry is definitely in the air with a friend or new acquaintance, isn't it appropriate to engage and explore that? am i the only one who enjoys this behavior? isn't it natural to feel butterflies and attraction and to act on them? as an adult, a single adult, able to make these distinctions even knowing that the person they are conversing with isn't 'the one' but could be for the night or many other random or selective nights to come?

if i am going to have sex with someone, it is because they mean something to me, that we have a connection. we are all connected and from an energy standpoint, and when a man inserts himself into a woman or however you prefer, it is an exchange of energy. it's almost as if we as women are an electrical outlet and they are 'plugging themselves into us.' and it is that exchange of energy that feels so right and so good and leads to an explosion (hopefully on both parts). there is nothing wrong with this behavior. and especially if you are communicating honestly and respectfully as well as being safe and consensual, where everyone knows what's going on, all should be well in the world. and just because you have sex doesn't mean that it needs to turn into a relationship.

it really depends on where each individual is. i know for the past several years i haven't been in the right frame of heart to be able to be with someone else at that level. only until recently have i healed from my past to be able to be open to actually being with someone else. and, because i am a special human being, (just as everyone one of us is) it's going to take a lot of someone who is equally as fabulous as i am (because i want and deserve an equal), to even penetrate my wall of relationshipdom. but that doesn't mean that in the mean time of finding that special someone that i'm going to be celibate. and who knows, maybe some day i'll choose that. so in an effort to keep a happy, healthy, relationship with myself, i have meaningful, honest connections with people who i communicate with openly.

as long as everyone is on the same page and everyone feels the same way, all is well. if not, or feelings change, then a conversation is had. i haven't really had to go there, because we were both honest in the first place. we continue to be. we don't want anything serious, but we really enjoy being around each other and would like to do dinners or drinks or dance, and maybe eventually lay with one another. ultimately it is because we are connected and genuinely do care for one another. and because of that, we wouldn't jeopardize the other persons health or safety, again, because we care about them.

so instead of having meaningless sex and conversation, why don't you find someone that you can gel with and then enjoy them as a human and love on them? that is ultimately what we are meant to do. we are depriving ourselves from rich, amazing experiences. and they do say that you've never met a stranger. isn't it strange how sometimes you connect with people so easily? like you've met them before? perhaps a previous life? there are plenty of people in this lifetime that i have recognized from a previous life. and if this sounds crazy, i've only come into this frame of mind recently. it is all new and remarkable to me. i invite you to join…

the break up

on the flip side of coming together is breaking apart. it was one day right before my daughter left for college, that i realized that my daughter and i were in the break up phase. we were fighting about stupid shit, really stupid shit, like the kind of stuff you fight about when it is time to break up with someone. at the end of one of my yoga sessions, as i was falling back into shavasana, i burst into tears. i couldn't keep it together, so i went outside the studio and let it all out. i cried for about fifteen minutes. then i came back inside and meditated for thirty minutes. afterwards, i knew what i had to do, so i went home and i told my daughter that we needed to talk.

she looked at me like someone died and i thought 'pretty much, we did.' i took her hands in mine and looked into her eyes and confessed 'i love you more than anyone else in this entire universe, but you are breaking my heart and shattering my soul and i can no longer do this. and all i want to do is help you and i am failing miserably. so i am breaking up with you, we can still be friends. i will always be your mother, as i always have, and will always be here for you, as i always will be, but i can no longer do this.' there was a moment of pause and then she looked at me and said, 'it's all my fault. i've been a complete shit. i'm sorry' and we embraced. i wanted to shake the shit out of her and say 'fuck yes you have' but instead i just squeezed her tight and loved upon her.

following that conversation, her verbiage immediately changed towards me. my mother (among others) asked if i kicked her out. i said, 'no. we just needed to verbally break up.' i think most parents physically break up with their kids when they go off to school, i just didn't want us to have a bad time leading up to her going away to college and wanted to talk about it before i dropped her off for a few weeks/months. i wanted to have a great relationship with my daughter. so we discussed it and faced it before she left for school. of course she resorted back to some of the bullshit, but we had met our next transition of our relationship. if you think about a cycle, that was just us coming up on ours.

she was transitioning from being a teenager to an adult. it was time the course of our communication changed. and to not permanently break up with my child, we embraced the change and let go of the past so we could move forward. all relationships are meant to move forward. it's when they stop or go backwards that they are no longer serving you. and i only now wish that i could have recognized that in my previous relationship, but i wasn't in that place. glad we are where we are now. we both needed the time.

i admire people who have been married or in a partnership for years and they can gracefully recognize that they are both unhappy and although they love their partner, they are no longer serving them, therefore one releases the other. we are meant to let go. it takes strength. it's 'easier' to stay. but isn't it only prolonging the inevitable? and wouldn't it be great if you could salvage this amazing friendship that you have with someone that you love before it becomes bitter, before someone cheats on someone else, before one completely compromises themselves to try to make themselves fit into this relationship leaving them resentful and angry.

side note, i read something somewhere that when you are living in anger and resentment, you're living in the past. when you live in fear or anxiety, that's the future. when you're in the present, you're in bliss. because what has happened has already happened. and what hasn't happened, hasn't fucking happened yet. i could walk into the street tonight and get hit by a car and die. but the present, the present is the only thing we actually have. the right here, the right now. and most of the relationship things happen when we are all in our head and we let our mind get away and into the future or holding onto the past that we fuck things up.

anyway, back to my daughter and our break up. we needed the conversation to happen, but that doesn't mean that we're done having them. we continually grow and learn from each other how to communicate effectively because we both want to have a great relationship with each other. sometimes we just get into these habits that take a while to break. so imagine that it takes 66 (i thought it was 40) times to make a habit. does that mean 66 times to break them? so now translate that shit to every area of your life. working out, going sober, not reacting like normal to every situation based on our life's experiences. you have to be diligent, you have to commit, you have to work on it, you have to be aware of it, then you have to do something about it.

breathe and exhale

and to do that, you must breathe. silly that something so simple that we do without thinking all day throughout the day, but seriously, consciously focusing on the breath will make a profound difference in your life. if this sounds stupid, i promise you, if you simply just pay attention to your breath, your life can magically change. you see, we all breathe, but when we get in certain situations, we inhale, but we hold in our breath. we don't exhale. breathing in is what most people do, but they forget that they need to expel that energy as much as they took into release. people forget, we are meant to release, we are meant to let go. we are designed this way.

there is an ebb and flow to everything. think about the breath, think about the ocean, think about expelling waste from our bodies, think about crying, think about having an orgasm. have you ever realized how we hold on so tightly to something and how toxic it becomes. we are all here to serve a purpose. many of them in fact as it pertains to interactions with humans, but when things become hard (and i don't mean you shouldn't have to work to be in a relationship), but getting into it should be easy, natural. if you're having problems off the bat, just walk away. the first three months you are meeting their representative anyway. isn't everyone on their best behavior to lure this other individual over?

well the secret is, that what you do in the beginning paves the path for expectations down the road. if you are full of shit and aren't being yourself, you are basically conning the person to be with you. which is fucked up. and actually, you are conning yourself. you should just be yourself in the first place and if the person isn't digging your vibe, then they aren't your person. don't waste your time and don't try to convince them to be with you. do you realize how fucked up that is too? you should just be your natural self as they should be too, and if it works, awesome, if not, no worries. love and learn and let go…

also on this journey of life, i learned about my dosha. a dosha is one of three substances that are present in a person's body according to ayurveda, the traditional hindu system of medicine, while based on the idea of balance in bodily systems and uses diet, herbal treatment, and yogic breathing. the quality and quantity of these three substances fluctuate in the body according to seasons, time of day, diet, and several other factors. the central concept is that health exists when there is a balance between the three fundamental bodily bio-elements or doshas called vata, pitta, and kapha.

vata is characterized by the properties of dry, cold, light, minute, and movement. all movement in the body is due to properties of vata. pain is the characteristic feature of deranged vata. some of the diseases connected to unbalanced vata are flatulence, gout, rheumatism, etc. vata is not to be interpreted as air.

pitta represents metabolism. it is characterized by heat, moistness, liquidity, sharpness and sourness. its chief quality is heat. it is the energy principle which uses bile to direct digestion and enhance metabolism. unbalanced pitta is primarily characterized by body heat or burning sensation and redness.

kapha is the watery element, it is characterized by heaviness, coldness, tenderness, softness, slowness, lubrication, and the carrier of nutrients. it is the nourishing element of the body. all soft organs are made by kapha and it plays an important role in the perception of taste together with nourishment and lubrication.

doshas are the forces that create the physical body. they determine conditions of growth, aging, health, and disease. typically, one of the three doshas predominates and determines one's constitution or mind-body type. by understanding individual habits, emotional responses, and body type, practitioners can adapt their yoga practice accordingly. the same applies for ayurveda treatments focused on alleviating any doshic excesses (illness) via powerful herbs and/or through the improvement of general lifestyle practices such as pranayama, meditation and yoga postures.

there are clear indications when there exists an excess of a dosha, throwing the system off balance. for example, with excess vata, there can be mental, nervous and digestive disorders, including low energy and weakening of all body tissues. with excess pitta, there is toxic blood that gives rise to inflammation and infection. with excess kapha, there is an increase in mucus, weight, edema, and lung disease, etc. the key to managing all doshas is taking care of vata, as it is the origin of the other two.

i got all of that from wikipedia. hopefully that helps. anyway, part of this breathing and exhaling and mind.body.soul. journey is taking in all of this information to try to make me the best me i can be. omg that rhymed. anyway it can help you too...

silent meditation

exactly a year ago today, i engaged in a silent meditation. ironic, but not really. at the time i thought that i might explode from not talking, but alas, that did not happen. funny enough, i had taken myself away to the umstead (the only four star hotel in the area) to use a gift card i received seven months ago for my birthday, but since i had been sick, i haven't been able to go. i chose this weekend a few months back at the recommendation of my acupuncturist, who i haven't introduced yet, who told me to take more time for myself. but i digress...

a year ago i decided that i needed to be more grounded. well, i'd been recommended this too by my spiritual guide, but that was years prior. however the day before this silent meditation, i met with him for a past life regression. it was discovered that i was a native american male shaman 400 years ago. anyway, i thought it would be a good thing to do. to reflect. to sit in silence. to honor my deceased husband, and to honor myself. i felt driven to do it. so, at the better judgement of my other self, i went. i was not able to speak from friday at 5:30pm-sunday at 2pm.

no phone, no music, no verbal communication to the outside world. mind you, this was the weekend before my eight year anniversary party and fashion show that i mandated we have a month prior. so i met friday, saturday, and sunday for hours to listen, to experience, to move. i remember walking home the first night with my notepad and running into someone that lived in my building and he asked me about my show and i had to hold up my pad that read 'i am going through a silent meditation.' that was hard.

the next morning i went on a walk around cameron park. i noticed nature more than i had in a long time. as i passed a man, he said 'good morning' and all i could do was smile really wide and bright, but i felt awful not being able to resend anything to him verbally. thank god our paths crossed again on the way back and i was able to show him my message of being on a silent meditation. however the practice of being silent was actually not that hard. i didn't miss my phone. i didn't explode. i made it. and when i was done, i realized that i wanted more of that- silence, nature, not at the beck and call of my phone. it was peaceful. that's when i started reading again.

i am currently in the middle of reading seven books, something i never thought i would do, as i'm usually a 'one at a time' person. but lately i have this unquenchable thirst for knowledge and find myself reading all the time. i've missed this. what a novel and sad approach. why is it that we are constantly finding ourselves doing something and not just sitting and relaxing? why do we feel like we have to be connected and jump every time our phone makes a noise. i implore all of you, take some time to just be. we all tend to use these things as distractions. that's what you realize once you do a silent meditation.

that all these things are keeping your emotions and feelings at bay. when we get overwhelmed, we go to our phones to get distracted. we get in a fight, so we yell and scream and shut down. when things get stressed we watch something to escape our reality. the reality is, these things don't go away, they just get buried. if you never unpack the baggage, it's just going to build up and eventually explode. that's why taking the time to reflect and deal with these issues are paramount to our physical health. all this heaviness weighs us down. what we don't realize is that once we expose the truth, which sometimes can be painful, it will set us free. and that will cause us all to breathe a little easier.

but before i so lightly step off of the beaten path of the silent mediation, when i did come back to my phone, i had 45 texts and 45 emails. and i handled it in 45 minutes. no reason for any of us to be consumed by our phones that much. i realized i need more of that. now, a year later, i realized i haven't done enough of that at all. damn. so 66 times, right?

acupuncture w/ dr. jesus and little kendra

on my extensive journey through trying to find myself and peace through mind, body, soul, i finally took the advice of probably the fifth person who told me to try acupuncture. she told me about her acupuncturist and she called him dr. jesus. i thought, why not. i am not a fan of needles, or anything that inflicts physical harm, so i've always thought acupuncture wasn't for me. i was wrong.

when i came into the his office, i sat down and he asked me why i was there. i told him of my physical body pain, that i had been getting massages for over 22 years. also told him about my 4-11 yoga classes per week and getting chiropractic care for over the past year due to a botched headstand. i told him that everyone says i'm the strongest woman they know. i told him all about my daughter and her father and my father and my life. owning my own boutique and my power to gain world domination by taking over the universe. i told him of my responsibilities, my desires, my quest for peace.

he then asked me, so who are you now? like, what else after that layer is shed? after everything else was gone, i was just a tired, scared little girl wanting someone to hold me, tell me everything was going to be okay, and take care of me for once. he then introduced me to little kendra. my soul. and how she feels neglected and that i need to strengthen my connection with her to heal my body. i felt like i was on the right track. he also referenced a four part painting behind him which was an image of a tree going through four seasons. everything must bloom, so it can blossom, then it must fall, harvest, and rest, to be able to get up and go again. that is life. but we must feed our soul at every stage. and once we're connected to that part of ourselves, that is when we flourish.

before the initial session, i filled out a questionnaire asking all about my physical health, and medical history. i described my eating and drinking habits, among other things, that would help paint a picture of me on paper as it pertains to my overall body and how it functions. it was also at this time we started talking about my body, and how i was on fire most of the time. i had just found out my dosha last year and how that affects my body temperature and how to control through diet and exercise. maybe i was doing too much hot yoga. also liking really spicy foods, (more jalapenos please!) anyway, we talked about all that too.

after the therapy session, i got on the table. he had me face up and cover up with two towels. he gave me a handheld device to hold while he touched parts of my body with another handheld device. at each point, it would measure and after doing a body scan with that tool, he showed me what wasn't aligned and what was. apparently my liver and kidneys aren't in a good place. but of course that's connected to something else. anyway, after my diagnosis, he started putting tiny needles at certain points. i always asked him to explain what they were connected to, and he would tell me. he would always be so gentle especially when i would feel a zap. but he always put them in the exact right places. i could feel it. the intensity, the surge- i could feel energy traveling through me like a current flowing through my veins.

after releasing my fire (i literally envisioned tiny bits of steam pouring out of my body at each entry point) and moving energy through my entire body- oh and i forgot to mention he put another needle in my third eye in the middle of my forehead that blew my mind and then he left the room. he was gone for about ten to fifteen minutes. and i just laid there with several needles in my body so i couldn't move, and then, there was little kendra. there was also the sound of the ocean playing in the background, so that helped. i was relaxing! something that was very difficult for me to do. laying still doesn't exist in my world unless i am in bed sleeping. well, maybe except for massages and yoga, but you know what i mean. otherwise i'm operating at a very high frequency.

it was wonderful how i felt things churning in my body and throughout. i individually went to each one in my head and tried to connect to the point of entry and how my body was being affected. i was breathing in to them. everything was heightened. he came back in the room just as i felt like i could fall asleep. he asked me how i was and took out each and every needle. i felt like my world had just been rocked. i set up sessions every week for the next three weeks leading up to my birthday, then he was going on vacation after that, so we would reconvene. that night as i got into my car, i asked little kendra what she wanted to do. and i listened.

i'm still practicing this self care months later and still learning to listen to little kendra. i get all caught up the craziness of the mind and let it take me down the rabbit hole. each time you get out of it though, you feel a little closer to where you need to be. and we are all exactly right where we need to be right here, right now. trust yourself, do the work, and listen to your inner voice. that will lead you to your purpose.

reiki release and the black panther

leading up to my fortieth, which i was really excited about, i was focusing relentlessly on my mind, body, and soul. in addition to yoga, talk therapy, and chiropractic care, and now, acupuncture, i also was getting massages on a more regular basis. my massage therapist asked if she could practice doing reiki on me. wikipedia says reiki is a form of alternative medicine called energy healing. reiki practitioners use a technique called palm healing or hands-on healing through which a "universal energy" is said to be transferred through the palms of the practitioner to the patient in order to encourage emotional or physical healing. i was open, so i agreed. this was two days after receiving acupuncture for the first time that i had my appointment. since everything had been stirred up two days prior, this seemed like a good time to go.

upon my arrival, we sat and talked about what i wanted to release from me. one word fell out- my daughter's father name. she asked me for a word that would describe what i wanted to release and of course that word was pain. she asked me to stand up and she told me to repeat the words after her '(insert his name here), i release you.' as soon as i finished saying those words, she, with a large stone in her hand, cut an 'x' in front of my entire body. i felt a wave of energy flow through me and rock my system. then she stood to the right of me and we repeated the words and the 'x.' it was like i was spider woman and had a zap that shot out through both of the tops of my wrists. she went to the back of me and we did it again. this time from the tip of my head, all the way down my spine, over my ass, and shooting out of my heels, another jolt of energy shot through my system. lastly, on my left side, we completed the ritual and an entire wave from head to toe gently rocked my body. and then he was gone.

i immediately felt like i had a new body. all the pain that i had been carrying in my shoulders for the past 20+ years was gone. it was like magic. i moved over to the massage table and was asked to grab a crystal that spoke to me. not one quite did, and just as i was about to settle and go for a certain rock, she said, 'no, you need this one. this is the goddess stone.' i was like, 'alright…' i laid down on the bed and she told me to put it down where i felt like i should. i'm now writing this months later and as i was feeling that i immediately put it on my heart, i think i may have put it on my root chakra, my lower abdomen.

she started the process again. silently, she moved her hands above and around me, then on me. a perfect cocktail of massage and reiki, she explained that i would be going on a journey. as my eyes were closed i imagined myself as a black panther-

oh wait, side note. i must first tell you the story of when i got back from vegas in february. i hurt so bad, i begged to see my massage therapist the day i returned. when she flipped back the sheet, she told me my spine was fucked. i knew it already. i could feel it. during this quick massage of 60 minutes, she gave me one hell of a fucking massage. after that amazing rub down, she told me that she felt a black panther come out of me, etc. i was like, 'um whatever, but cool.' the very next day she sent me an article about how the black leopard, otherwise known as the black panther just revealed herself for the first time in 100 years to a photographer in africa. holy shit. anyway, had a moulin rouge dance party at the alamo, so i had to split. another great story, but i made my point…

so as i was imagining myself as a black panther going on this journey while i was laying on the table, i imagined i was walking in the middle of this thick jungle. and as i was walking i could feel my shoulders walk like a panther's does, and with that movement really unwinding my shoulders and i was making my way through. like breaking in my blades, or growing new wings. then, as i was walking through the jungle, it was getting less thick, more clear. then, eventually, out of me, my goddess self emerged. i was naked, walking next to the black panther. my hand gently grazed it as we walked in tandem. and there were vines in my hair and warrior paint on my arms, and legs, along with cuffs on my wrists and a choker on my neck.

but watching myself from the back, i thought, 'that's not my ass.' but as my eyes followed upwards towards my hair, it was long, almost to my ass, and wavy as it naturally is, and holding my warrior goddess weapon. shit, need to tell you another story first though...

so i told you i was doing all of this leading up to my fortieth, like weeks before. also weeks before my birthday, a client, who had only been in once before, came in to give me a gift. i was so surprised. and i'm not usually a big gift person, it's definitely not my love language, but i was really excited about it. again, as i am typing this months later, i imagined that it was in a black bag, wrapped in black tissue paper, then a black box. i opened the box (or now I'm questioning that- this is why you write shit down immediately) and inside there was a twisted black horn attached to a silver bottle opener. it was shiny and sharp, twisted to a point. and it felt good to hold, almost like it belonged to me. my client was very nervous giving it to me. and i was so grateful for this gift.

i literally walked around with that piece on my person for at least a week. i couldn't help it. it was calling to me. i needed to have it near me, in my hand, and carried it everywhere i went. not in a weapon way, but it did feel like it was some sort of protection. i called it my new toy. anyway, back to my experience...

so, in my hand walking through this jungle is my warrior goddess weapon. i'm tearing back the leaves as we walked together and cleared our path. just large gentle sways of my arms going through my path. things kept getting more clear the further we walked, and eventually i came to an open space. around this same time, the panther morphed into me. now, the whole time that this spiritual journey was happening, we were listening to drumming music. oh- side note, after the 'X' was cut across me, she drummed around me too. each time releasing more energy. anyway, as i turned over on the table, the spotify kinda went like a dj's hands would (can't think of how to type that sound) and the music turned into fleetwood mac's *dreams*.

'so they say you want your freedom...' and i walked into the meadow. there was this waterfall in the distance. and as i stepped inside this waterfall *'as the rain washes you clean you'll know'* poured over my soul. after several moments in the waterfall, i finally left it behind and walked out. the song switched to india arie's song *'i am light'* came on. and as the water evaporated off my body in the sunshine, i felt like light was beaming out

of me. kinda felt like the matrix light shining through. it was pouring out of me. then my experience was over. it was time to get up and move on…

funny thing is that my healer asked me to tell her what happened on my 'journey.' but before i could answer her, she told me that she saw everything happen as it did- the jungle, the black panther, the goddess, the clearing, the meadow, the waterfall. she knew everything i experienced without me even telling her. after this spiritual venture, i felt like a new version of myself.

the intuitive experience with
eve and cleopatra

a week after that happened, i had my second acupuncture appointment followed by meeting with an intuitive. i had met her previously at the yoga studio on many a mornings and we chatted briefly one time about what she did and what i did and somehow i mentioned my late husband and she said, 'that's why i need to see you.' i had always been intrigued, but never set anything up. well, after my reiki experience, my healer had mentioned she was meeting her friend who was an intuitive, and just like that, it was her. so, i decided it was now time. i came into her beautiful home and she offered me some tea. we spoke for a bit and she asked why i was here, and i told her all the things that i've been telling you.

she then asked if i wanted to record the conversation, and i did. super helpful to now go back and listen to that. also recently listened to all of my readings this year. such a great perspective to go back six months plus to listen and learn from those experiences. quite amazing too, since all that has transpired since then. anyway, she told me that she was feeling a major presence in the room as it pertained to me. she inquired if it was isis. it wasn't. then finally, she said 'oh my god. it's eve. the mother of all creation. she is totally supportive of this divine eroticism and power not for manipulation or control, but for love.'

she envisioned me with two golden shiny cuffs covering my arms but openings so that i could use my elbows. that was my armor. she said she felt as if there was a yoke or a breastplate, too. the yoke was gold and it had a very regal aspect and controlling aspect to it. ethereal. i carried it into this lifetime. and i somehow have embraced the energy when i wore it before, but it used to be rigid and controlling and done in love but was put in place by a previous lover, perhaps my ex. i had been bound and controlled. somewhat of a sex slave that needed to be healed and integrated and released in order to embrace this divine eroticism. fear from bondage and control from all the sex and force in my previous lives, or so i was told. a lot if made sense as i have always been terrified of physical pain. i'm sure i have been burned alive, quartered, hung, and physically tortured in my previous lives.

because i am an empath, i can pull that energy from my partners so i then have to clear that energy by having a sacred cleansing ritual with intention in my womb, to bless, honor, and love, where there is zero violation of the body so that i am only me in my field and no one else. i have this ancient connection. it has not been good in previous lives. my ex and i come in to do really great work together. he was very controlling in the past and there was no intention for me to be with him long term according to her. it wasn't a good supportive relationship for me into the past. it never has been positive apparently. it has been powerful, passionate, but too fiery. it's like fire with fire. too much conflicting emotion surrounding insecurity and jealousy. it derails my life. but i loved him and i know that we are soul mates, just not meant to be life partners.

i also had a life contract with my daughter's father. i was to learn boundaries and manipulation. to learn early in life. helpful to say 'not that' ever again. he was my early warning system. my best teacher. because i have things to do. i have shit to do. i have a big life to live and i don't need be swirling in this. or to lose that time with old shit. apparently in my past lives, my daughter has been my mother. many times, in fact. and this is the first time i've been her mother. why is she so opinionated about my life? why does she think she knows better? why is she so controlling? our contract is for her. to teach her compassion, love, kindness, and understanding. the two of us have agreed that i would be her mother in this lifetime. i am here to show her love. she is a big space. she wants to fix me and shape me. and i have to have her understand why she has been feeling this way, it's because she's been my mother. it's not personal. my daughter was the one who could get to little kendra.

as with eve, there is this energy going. she is helping me see things very clearly so that i have this undistracted force of energy with which to manifest my dreams in the world. this is an unusually powerful directive session and it is very clear. it's a big time for forward movement. in this lifetime i do not wear a collar. (though i do were a choker most days). it's my life on my terms. she is me. eve unleashed. i'm not great at discerning people who aren't good for me. knowing who to trust in life. who has my back and who doesn't. it's all residue from the breast plate. the oppression of the female. i completely accept this game of confusion of conflict and control. i have managed to carry this breast plate for so long and have been this successful because of the transgressions and oppressions of the past.

this controller keeps me going, keeps me strong, but i would not have made it this far without my controller. it can be overprotective. it's afraid of how free i'm going to be. it has to realize that i am trustworthy. it's control is an illusion. it needs to release me. she's a few paces ahead of me controlling the experiences. keeping people at bay that may be threatening to ultimately protect me. learning my own discernment. my male energy is experiencing this contrast to heal, shift, and grow. this masculine and feminine energy flow and it's a love affair. it's all about my voice, boundaries, all about not being triggered, and stepping up and getting very clear. very focused.

part of the focus is in this sexual energy stemming from cleopatra, the debauched temptress who used her sex appeal as a political weapon. but some claim that her beauty was not altogether incomparable, and that it was instead her mellifluous speaking voice and irresistible charm that made her so desirable. she knew how to make an entrance as she believed herself to be a living goddess. she was also referred to as a woman of insatiable sexuality and avarice. interaction with her was captivating, and her appearance, along with her persuasiveness in discussion and her character that accompanied every interchange, was stimulating. but in a world driven by such fear, cleopatra was driven by absolute passion. she wanted what she wanted, and would do anything to get it. this is a woman who i've been compared to over the last several years.

so lessons i've learned from this cleopatra energy that i possess that i wish to pass onto you: don't be afraid to admit to yourself what you truly desire. know who you need to persuade to get what you want. humans think in terms of stories, so use a bit of theatrics to gain an edge. package your introductions in such a way that would make for a powerful story for powerful people. cleopatra was not known for her compassion, but she did exhibit a high degree of empathy, one of my many strengths as well. persuasion is about understanding the wants/desires/values/fears of your audience. help people get what they want so you can get what you want. become more scholarly. my name means knowledgeable. and knowledge is power. and powerful people like interesting people, but to be interesting, one must first be interested. roll out the red carpet.

my fortieth

so, the moment that i had been waiting for, my fortieth birthday. i went to work and felt absolutely amazing. a gentleman who i had met the week prior called me and asked if he could witness my business as he knew nothing of retail and wanted to see me in action. you see, he just so happened to stumble upon my store and after chatting for an hour, i felt compelled to ask him if he wanted to give me a million dollars so i could open a store or two. he questioned my question, and i told him that i just felt like he was the type of person who could make something like that happen. and he said, 'i like you. you remind me of me.'

so when he just so happened to call on my birthday not knowing it was such, i said 'sure thing! it's my birthday! i've gotten six bouquets of flowers and getting hugs left and right. it's the perfect day for you to come and watch me work.' so he did. within a few minutes of him being there, i got a phone call from this guy in dc whom i hadn't spoken with in several months. he asked if i was still interested in dc, and i was like, 'sure, what do you have?' and he said 'so there's this place called the black cat' (remember the black panther?). and i was like, if that's not writing on the wall, i don't know what is. so he sent me this info and this investor guy stayed to watch and that was my amazing day at work. happy birthday to me!

after work, i went to dinner with my parter in crime and we made our way to my fabulous party. i had a doorman, a dj, a dancer, a red carpet, invited over 1,000 people and it was cocktail or black tie optional. i was stoked. one of my favorite things is to bring together people who would not ordinarily come together and mix them all up. i have such a diverse collection of amazing souls in my life, so all good energy surrounds me, therefore everyone else gets in on that too. so many people came and left and had a great time. i danced the entire night cause i had made three playlists and i kept clutching my heart, which is common for me to do as my heart feels so intently. this feeling was the overwhelming sense of love and affection that i felt for my friends and the love they shared in return.

lots of laughter, lots of love, a few tears of happiness, and a whole lotta dancing. it was a great night. it ended with an intimate after party at my place followed by more dancing and tears and meaningful conversation. oh, and three men massaging my feet by the end of the night. i must say, forty felt great. i was on top of the world. the next day was a saturday and i was able to celebrate that day too. started with a magnificent brunch, then onto walking through the city and traveling from one place to the next accompanied by adult water (otherwise known as vodka, soda water, and lime) throughout the process.

of course day drinking tends to hit you hard. i paused but continued on this forum throughout the evening and ended up with more dancing and late night conversation. that sunday i took myself out to brunch and was going to go read in the park, but my body was screaming at me to get that well deserved birthday massage. now i have mentioned that i have been getting massages for over 22 years. and generally, although i do get a ton of relief, it comes with a great deal of pain. so it wasn't uncommon for me to scream obscenities while all my knots were being released. i carry lots of stress in my neck and shoulders and throughout my legs. pretty much everything hurts.

that massage led into my demise of dehydration which led me to the hospital. out of nowhere my life came screeching to an undesirable halt. typing this up so nonchalantly seems very unsettling, but that is how life works, right? one minute, you're having the time of your life, living life to the fullest, going about your normal behavior, when all of the sudden death is knocking at your door for your poor decisions and making you question your lifestyle.

people have always questioned my age, especially when i tell them i have a twenty year old daughter, but i have always embraced it. in fact, i cannot wait to go grey. i'm excited. in fact, i want to live a long and very healthy life, which is why i have tried to incorporate things such as meditation, yoga, massage therapy, talk therapy, acupuncture, chiropractic care, and just recently added getting pedicures to my list. self care is not indulgent, it's necessary. letting yourself go and losing yourself to your partner, your work, your children, doesn't do anyone any good. you must take care of yourself and love upon yourself otherwise there is no chance of living a long, happy, healthy life.

they say your issues are in the tissues. thanks to *anatomy of the spirit* by caroline myss i have a much deeper understanding of the body and how what happens to you in life affects every part of you. the connection of the mind, body, and soul. meaning that whatever ailments you may be having physically, they are likely emotionally tied to trauma that you've had in your life. and how you deal with that trauma impacts how your body receives it and deals with it. so i encourage all of you, to take the time to reflect and heal yourself and past wounds so that you can start enjoying each and every day that you have been given as a gift. each day that you peel back the covers of your bed is like unwrapping your present of a brand new day. live each day like it's your last and love deeply. take care of your bodies and thank them for taking care of you. it's the only body you'll ever have.

after dealing with pneumonia, these are my take aways: the spiritual cause of pneumonia could be the result of a sudden traumatic event that happened in my life- i've had many. what ended up coming to the surface is a suppression of grief. the fear and anxiety around this could have left me with an overwhelming feeling of futility. there is a failure to maintain immunity to negative ideals, made worse by a strong ego, one that i am caught up in a conflict with, where there was little tolerance for other ideas or opinions. the reason may be due to being emotionally abandoned at a young age, resulting in the need to build up defenses which have not allowed people in and myself out. there has been a strong belief in having to deal with the world single-handedly. the end result is being put off from joy and love. it is a sign that the process of communication with life including the nonmaterial ones, is disturbed.

if we look deeper with those emotions and the spiritual cause of pneumonia and lung problems it also references a lack of inspiration, keeping out anything that is new. an inability to let go (exhalation), a fear of letting something die away. pneumonia can also relate to a fear of death or seeing someone else suffer or die, and extreme fear of change. lastly, someone or something might be taking my life-force away, resulting in the feeling of suffocation.

   my body has been trying to communicate my need to address certain internal emotions. when i refused to listen to my inner emotions, pneumonia, like any illness, my body was desperately trying to, literally express painful truths. believe me, now i'm listening. every ailment in your body can be linked to emotional trauma. if you find yourself having consistent patterns of behavior within how your body functions, pay attention. i think of my husband who had leukemia. this is cancer of the blood, it was everywhere. his disease was just as aggressive as he was. it came back with a vengeance and ended up taking his life.

   if you find yourself faced with some kind of illness or dis-ease, take a look at the meaning behind the surface of what is physically wrong with you and how it can be linked to your emotional pain. organs are linked to channels and systems within the body that are connected to the mind and your spirit is at the center. find your center.

be careful what you wish for

so with all of that being said, be careful what you wish for. or better yet, be mindful of what you put into the universe. the universe is listening, as well as your body. (remember the japanese rice experiment?) for years, and i'm talking years, i have been saying that i don't know how to relax. well, the universe gave me pneumonia and told me i had no choice. i also used to say things like, 'i just like to inhale.' well, after pneumonia i received this breathalyzing treatment to practice my inhaling to rebuild my lungs back to full capacity. not quite what i had in mind. this was my opportunity to breathe in the breath of life once again.

after the initial two weeks of being diagnosed, i thought i could go back to work. not the case. within the first few minutes of cleaning the store (a minor chore, by the way) i was light headed. i had to sit down. i didn't realize just how much energy it took to stand up, to move gently throughout the store. i also had a hard time communicating verbally. literally i had to take a break in between my words just to make it through an idea or thought. not the frequency i was used to operating under. it was very humbling.

but also really scary. i had many people tell me that i wouldn't go back to being me and i might as well get used to this. that was absolutely terrifying. then i had others encourage me that in a few months i would be absolutely back to my normal self and just needed to take this time to rest. and that is exactly what i did. so i learned how to sit still, which was completely foreign to me. i woke up, and sat. and read. and started writing. i introduced myself and others to poolside meetings. i strongly encourage more people to meet outdoors. where i live, we have lots of vegetation and running jets so the sound of water and being surrounded in nature was so very peaceful. and necessary. during this transition i came to realize how nice it was to be surrounded by trees and feeling water at my feet, as well as planting my feet in mother earth.

being in my industry, i dress every day. well, i've been dressing since i can remember, but part of that also required shoes to be on my feet. my spiritual guide suggested that i needed to ground more considering my head is always swimming in the clouds and simply walking on the grass can be incredibly therapeutic. or simply standing in the sand. as i was healing there was a time when i felt like i was being broken down to the cellular level and being built back up and all the weight was in my ankles, heels, and feet. they were so heavy. simply picking them up and putting one foot in front of the other was such a monumental task. and i guess if you think about it, it makes sense. i didn't have enough oxygen to disperse throughout my body. which is why i described pneumonia is complete weakness down to the bones. everything was labored.

but the days and weeks went on, and finally i came to feel back to myself once again. i got a new outfit and was feeling amazing. kendra 2.0. but a few days later, i woke up early in the morning and was going to have my morning tea when i went to scratch my stomach and it burned. i was wearing my silk robe and something that was so delicate and agreeable to the senses shouldn't have felt coarse and painful, but it did. i had six red bumps on my abdomen that weren't there the night before. my mother feared it was shingles, and she was right. apparently my immune system was still compromised and my stress led me to this wonderful little opportunity. fortunately i went to the doctor that day and got it under control before it took control of me.

you see, our bodies speak to us and if we just listen (and respond accordingly) we can catch things before they spin violently out of control. because i took immediate action, i received antibiotics that kicked it out immediately and i never had the crazy nerve pain or major itching symptoms normally associated with shingles. so many people that i have met throughout the course of my life felt like there was something wrong with them prior to finally breaking down and going to the doctor. and so many people want to live in denial of what is actually happening that they ignore their symptoms and mask it with certain behaviors which just prolongs the inevitable and allows the problem to get bigger. it's weird how we do that sometimes. but that's human nature.

the underlying emotional component of a virus is feeling hopeless and helpless. the blisters signifies resisting the flow of life, dreading a situation because it feels like no emotional protection is available. those thoughts show up as emotional eruptions on the body- blisters. the emotional component of nerve inflammation is referred to as an agitated irritation, something that happens when people feel like they're continually subjected to tension-inducing stimulation. the stress frustrates them; they feel powerless and undermined because of it. this all ties back to the thought pattern behind contracting shingles- namely, a generalized dread about a situation needing to be faced. not surprisingly, my need for nurturance, protection, and affection possibly dictated this. cause and effect.

i've recently been told that i make connections out of everything. and that maybe sometimes things just happen and there is no connection. i fail to believe this. maybe this is just my fantastical way of living in this life. of course i'm not ignorant to the negative side of things, but i choose to see the positive. i look for understanding to make sense of a certain situation. i really do believe that the universe listens to us and if we just simply listened back, we would all be living a better life. we constantly get signs thrown at us, but maybe those warning signs are there for a reason. maybe we chose to not listen, which is our free will, but all actions or inactions have an equal or greater consequence. maybe by simply listening to the universe aka spirit, source, god, etc. we are ultimately hearing our higher self call on us to be our best selves, driven with purpose and love.

but, if you've heard the adage from lao tzu, 'watch your thoughts, they become your words; watch your words, they become your actions; watch your actions, they become your habits; watch your habits, they become your character; watch your character, they become your destiny' it all makes perfect sense. our mind simply just says yes to everything we think- the good and the bad, and we start speaking these things to fruition. i'm a huge fan of this mantra. if you are not speaking the language and living the life you want to live, you are the one holding yourself back- no one else.

a line from shakespeare that says 'nothing is either good or bad, but thinking makes it so.' the important lesson here, an essential part of awakening of consciousness is to learn to become aware of the difference between the situation you find yourself in, and what your mind says about the situation you find yourself in. we are absolutely in control of our thoughts and emotions. even though most of us let them get the best of us. however no one can make you 'feel a certain way,' it's your way of processing what they did or said and how you are also projecting your viewpoint through their words. we tend to be each others mirrors then in essence, showing each other another aspect of ourselves that we may not have even known it existed.

all i'm trying to say here is to be aware of your thinking. negative thoughts, lead to negative words, to negative actions, etc. instead, flip the script. it's also important to note that we are creatures of habit. we tend to get stuck in our rut (way of thinking/doing) and it is hard to create new thought patterns or behaviors. however, if you catch yourself saying something you 'used to say all the time' and it has a negative connotation, switch it up. for example, i always used to say that my daughter's father was an asshole (i'm pretty sure he says the same about me), but now i have made the conscious effort to correct that speech to 'he was my greatest teacher.' you see, negative into a positive.

i'm not saying this is easy, it's not. it requires discipline, awareness, and open-mindedness. and again, the habits thing, it's gonna take some time, so be nice to yourself. just cause you mess up one day, doesn't mean that you can't try again later. breaking habits or changing your routine is hard. but, there is no time other than the present and right now you can make the choice to be happy, to change your behaviors, your words, your thoughts to become the absolute best version of yourself. it starts with you. no matter what has happened to you in your past, you can claim your future by living your present.

bali

i just booked my trip to bali last week. bali has been calling me for
months now. a place that really hadn't in the past. leading up to the trip
i was told that there was another silent meditation the weekend prior to
my leaving for bali. so once again, i will practice in silence before going
on my spiritual journey. i think that will be a great send off for me. silence
and stillness are great teachers to us and if we just listen, the messages
come through ever so clearly. and when they don't, just relishing in the
nothingness is okay, too. sometimes it really is just okay to sit and just be
with whatever is.

and as i am currently sitting with what is, i am officially in bali.
thank you, by the way for following along on my back and forth stories.
maybe that's why i like quentin tarantino so much because i understand
his timelines. anyway, leading up to this trip a lot has happened. i did just
finish that other silent meditation. i sat silent for another two and a half
days. i was going to read, work on my book, do laundry, and pack, but i
was advised to actually do nothing and just sit with my thoughts.

a lot came up for me. i got really clear about my business, my sexuality,
my absent father, my late husband, and my daughter. i had thoughts about
becoming celibate, selling my business, two things i never thought i would
ever think about doing. never say never, right? i love how life turns things
upside down for us. you never quite know what's about to be shaken up.
being that i was going to bali solo, i kinda continued the silence. i wasn't
completely silent or off the grid, but i was in my head. i continued to
journal as i had done during the silent mediation, something that i have
been wanting to do more of. i also realized my eyes have gone to shit along
with my handwriting, so i need to practice writing more as opposed to
typing and i officially had to get glasses to read, be on my computer, and

drive at night. they say 2020 is the year of perfect vision. apparently 40 is a magical age…

so, bali. bali is beautiful. when i booked this trip suddenly, all i knew was that i was looking for peace and quiet, calm. i found it. the place i am staying is surrounded with vegetation- trees are everywhere, the grass seems extra green. it has great feng shui. i found out the owner actually hired chinese designers to construct the entire grounds to ensure that peace and serenity as it pertains to the flow of energy. after my silent meditation, i felt so incredibly clear, so grounded. weird coming from my fantastical pisces self always swimming in the clouds.

the journey over seemed effortless. also strange for a 30 hour flight package. i arrived in the afternoon and went for a two hour stroll. ended up with a margarita in my hand listening to a balinese band singing cover songs. the next two days were lazy days for me on the beach, hiding underneath an umbrella of course. don't know if i mentioned that i'm a vampire and cannot be exposed to sunlight. seriously. i have hyperpigmentation, a condition which i have dealt with since after i gave birth to my daughter 20 years ago. i was a sun goddess back in the day. i used to get super dark and live in the sun. that all changed and now i get frecklefied every time my face is exposed to the sun. i originally cut bangs due to the shape of china growing on my forehead.

after two days of lounging, and about two hours of walking each night in each direction, i decided to venture out, well, to the other side. the following day i walked around the streets of bali all day. i shopped a little, but i wasn't really in that mindset. also, tourist traps are not for my liking. i did encounter a bunch of random souls with amazing smiles as i walked down the streets of bali. for such a beautiful place, it is a shame at how incredibly dirty it was. i knew it was a third world country, but i guess i made an assumption (something i desperately need to work on) that it would be cared for more properly based on what i knew about the culture. but what do i know. i know nothing.

the next day was sunday and i had arranged a day trip to ubud. when i got picked up, i was informed things had changed. but change is good. i was taken to see a shaman although i was supposed to do this the following day after riding an elephant. so over the river and through the woods, we made our way to the son of the shaman who met with elizabeth gilbert, author of *eat, pray, love*. his father had died three years prior, at the age of 103, and due to ancient balinese tradition, his father's wisdom and role was passed onto him. so i entered his home, watched him pray and go through a series of rituals, before he summoned me.

before he took my hands into his, he told me not to worry about anything ever again, no stress. immediately after he took my hand, he said i was going to live a long and healthy life and have much success. he said i was pretty, very healthy and very smart, but i have forgotten to pray. if i'm patient, balanced, and confident, i will have luck every day of my life. i have positive thinking, and that will take me far. however, my financial struggle is real. i need to save more. so glad i booked an appointment with a financial advisor as soon as i return from my trip. he said if i can save more, i'll be more lucky. he also said my long life line was a symbol of success, that i lived life right. well, i'm working on it. he said the gods have blessed me. that i was 40, and i would not be young again, and i would have blessings for the next 20 years.

he told me i needed to be happy more, be happy now. that i will be very popular. that as a professional, people would come to me. i need to have a business alone. i would be better alone than in a company. i have luck, long life, health, but economic trouble. lovely. easy come, easy go. go figure. i need to eat three meals a day. be disciplined and responsible. i have a very strong heart line, strong personality, as long as i do not lose my heart, i will love again. must choose the best partner- the most handsome, healthy, happy, otherwise i am better off single. i have artistic talent, this is my purpose, and i need to do the best quality. due to my professionalism and my gifts, people will come to me. still have one child inside of me. jesus. better not. though i'm hoping that just means i'll just put my arm around someone else's. my chakras are completely clear. woohoo! i am lucky, but i need to be patient, and balanced. he said his wife picked a yellow flower for me. he said not everyone likes yellow, but yellow means success. i will only do positive work based on this symbol.

he then put rice on my forehead, had me stand up, which at this point, both of my feet had fallen asleep. so remember when i said that i felt like my feet were so heavy and i needed to plant my feet in mother earth? well as they were tingling so intensely, i felt like this was all the residual crap leaving my system and as he was pouring water over my head, it was another feeling of being free, cleansed, and reborn. i had been going through a death process for months, feeling compelled to cut all my hair off, just like i did when my husband died ten years ago. it was this overwhelming feeling that it needed to be gone. nothing on my neck, no hair for anyone to grab, literally cut it loose and let it go. another symbol.

lastly, he tied a bracelet around my wrist. three strings in one, twisted, symbolizing the three gods in one, also, symbolizing the three phases of our fate- birth, life, and death. of course it makes me think of mind, body, soul. the white was for spirituality and goodness, red symbolizes creativity and bravery, and black symbolizes power and protection. that got me thinking to my way of dressing. you see, i'm mostly in black. black on black and then more black. i've recently discovered that the reason i've been wearing black is for power and protection. i never really thought about it, but it makes sense. hence the black panther. i was protecting my heart. black was my armor, covering me up, protecting me from the outside world, from getting hurt, exposed, being completely vulnerable. now i have a reminder and know that i am strong enough and have healed over this time.

the following day i got to hang out with elephants. if you ever get the chance to spend time with these amazing creatures, please do. this, in addition to my reading, was definitely the highlight of my trip. i got to feed them, and one was actually dancing which was an awesome sight to see. when it was my turn to go for a ride, my elephant in queue came up, the people who were riding him got off, and instead of waiting for me, the elephant walked away. i was like, 'wait?!' but when i turned to look back at the next elephant that was approaching the loading deck, i noticed it was huge. it just so happened to be the largest elephant in the entire park. when i got on him, his trainer who had been with him 6 days a week since 1997 told me that i got the best one. i felt like the queen of the jungle. the next day was my last to relax and enjoy so i took the day in as much as possible. then it was time to leave. i made my way through the airport, bought another journal cause mine was almost filled up and picked up another book, *the power of the subconscious mind* by joseph murphy. started reading it while waiting for my flight to dubai.

after i arrived in dubai, i got a latte, journaled, and read some more. after getting to the lower level to leave for nyc, we had another security check. the gentleman asked me if i had any electronics in my bag, and of course, i went to get my laptop. well, i should take the time to tell you that i only travel with a carry on suitcase. of course, i had an oversized beach bag filled to the brim with things (my floppy hat, my books, my journals, my laptop, my toiletries, an extra pair of shoes, etc.) and when i went to check in for my flight in bali, they took my carry on, cause my 'personal item' was rather large. so this backfired and i had to lug my huge bag throughout bali, dubai, and nyc. nothing i could do, though, so i moved on.

so when i went to pull my laptop out of my bag and it wasn't there, i started to panic. you see, kendra leonard doesn't lose things. and so as i was standing there in disbelief, and realizing that my laptop was gone. and it wasn't really that my laptop was gone, it was more that i had been working on my book while i was in bali, and since it wasn't backed up (cause i'm computer illiterate- need to stop saying that too) my book was gone. it was at this time that i looked at my watch and knew that there was no way of my going back to the airplane before my flight left in an hour. so i had an 'oh shit moment,' and then i let it go.

that's right, i completely let it go. maybe my book wasn't supposed to be read after all. the gentleman told me to go see another man who gave me the info to make a claim. he also called someone about it cause i thought for sure it must have fallen out of the overhead compartment. they couldn't find it, but he assured me that it would turn up and i would get it back in a few days. that comforted me, but i was still breathing heavily and trying to calm myself down. so i went ahead and made the claim, and got out my book to work on this mind over matter stuff. but i couldn't concentrate. so i stood up and went to the corner to practice some yoga and meditation to breathe my way through this.

and it worked. by the time i got on the plane, i had completely let it go. cause there was absolutely nothing i could do about it. i could swirl and do the what if's and where, but it did me no good to go down this road. it was gone. i did have fourteen hours to think about things on the way back home, and it was only then that i wondered, 'what if it never made it to the plane or to dubai?' i talked to about eight people among the three airports and they all said that this happens all the time and it would turn up. a few days after my arrival, i received an email stating that they still had not found it. i tried reaching out to the dubai and balinese airports, but never heard back.

every week or so, i would reach out to ask them, and i would get nada. finally a friend suggested that i reach out to the resort i stayed at for more help. then, almost a month to the day later, i got an email. they found my laptop!!!!!!!! i could not believe that it turned up! i completely released it and it came back to me! the day after my birthday, i was planning on driving to dc to pick it up as emirates didn't have a hub in raleigh and i needed to go look at another space in dc for my store as i also had released the black cat space, but we had this little thing called the coronavirus come up, so i decided to have them ship it. it had made it this far, what's one more little flight?

the current situation

my laptop arrived at my store on friday, march 20th, two months after i had left for bali. this was three days after i was forced by the government to shut the doors to my store due to the spread of the virus. it is now, friday, april 10th, and i am sitting here for the first time since bali, working on my book. everything in last few months has changed drastically. it is surreal. everything is shut down. bars and restaurants are closed, no one is out and about. airports are empty, uber and airbnb have shut down, a stay at home order has been issued for most of the world where we can only go out for doctor's visits, pharmacy pick ups, and grocery store runs. the entire world is operating this way and has been for weeks. everyone is out of work, people are being laid off or furloughed. the government supposedly is going to send everyone some free money, but nothing has arrived yet. i've applied for everything i can, but to no avail. however, i am not worried.

you see, kind of like the laptop situation, there is nothing i can do about this. it is out of my control. and everyone is in the same situation, so it's not like i'm the only one. instead of living in the spiral of negativity and what if's, i choose to see this as a gift. this is the universe telling us to slow down. mother earth is healing. within just a few weeks of the world being shut down, the skies are clearing and the bodies of water are more clear, too. we have had an enormous impact on our planet but the way we have treated it is appalling. we were forced by mother nature to take this time to allow all of us to breathe/heal once again, so is she.

i have taken this time to appreciate nature even more. daily walks along with mediation and yoga and simply seeing the sky have done my body good. eating blocks of cheese, not so good. but we are experiencing something that is unprecedented. and we need to take a look at ourselves. be with ourselves. be grateful for the people in our lives and all the many (and sometimes unnecessary) things that we have. this situation has shaken most of us to our core. many of us are not working, some of us are quarantined with our families, some of us are working from home, some are home schooling, and some people like me are getting an opportunity to really focus on doing things differently.

there has definitely been a shift this year. back in january, my spiritual guide held a '2020 year in review' session. it was at this time that he said major shifts that no one could foresee were coming. he said we haven't seen the likes of these times since civil war and world war ii eras, which were dark times. that's where we are. but i am choosing to see what comes after those times: reinvention, rebirth, revitalization, refresh, reawaken, resuscitate, rehabilitate, and revolution.

so even when there seems like there is no end in sight, all will be well. all is well. the sun is shining, the weather has been exceptional. just like in true form, raleigh gets to experience all four seasons in a week. this situation is kind of like a death of a relationship. we are all getting a first glance at what our lives look like, what's most important, and how to make use out of this time. we collectively as a group of people are coming together and will get through this. years ago, when i made the jump to open my first store, i realized that the absolute worst thing that could happen would be that i died. and until then, i'm gonna keep going, and i'm not going out without a fight. so i am optimistic that my business will survive and soon be thriving once more.

don't get me wrong. when all this first started, i was definitely like 'wtf?' i could see death, darkness, despair, armageddon, zombie apocalypse, everything closed and shut down, riots, looting, etc. everyone's broke and can't work cause everything is shut down and no one is hiring. we're heading into a handmaid's tale type situation where martial law exists and the current president has become a dictator and eliminated the option for an election and has taken over the world so i will never again watch the news. but no. that is not going to happen. i have faith in humanity and the human spirit.

this is causing all of us to be creative at what we do and how we do it. what we really need and what we really want. turns out, i don't really 'need' anything. other than gas and groceries, i haven't spent money on anything in the last month. it's amazing that this is a modern day problem with long lasting impacts that will change the way we do things for the foreseeable future. hopefully we will come out of this stronger, more united as a collective whole. if we can turn inward and see all the beauty and gifts that lie within us and then reflect the light back into the world to share with others, we can and will change the world for the better. this is an opportunity for a fresh perspective, for a restart. it's like new year's eve all over again...or maybe more like groundhog day. you can make the choice to either change your habits to create better ones, or you can continue to run the rat race and stay on the wheel in the same situation. your choice. either way, it's a chance to learn, to grow, to be.

my point is, we all have a piece of the divine within us, and the connection that our minds, bodies, and souls have are our starting point. we literally have everything we need, all the time, at our disposal. we are the key to unlocking our our true purpose. quiet your mind, it likes to run around in circles. listen to your body, it's speaking to you constantly. search for your soul deeply, and make sure you're serving it first. lastly, you are the only you that exists in the entire universe (well, right now at least). so please, do your part and be the best you, that you can be. live every day like it's your last and look good while you're doing it...

afterword

a month and a half after this book was written and sent to be published, kendra's store got destroyed in the riots. in her attempt to heal and seek clarity, she went on a three month sabbatical to croatia and italy. another lesson in learning to let go and put herself first to be able to eventually serve others once again, kendra continues her journey of self exploration. while on her time away, she wrote what will eventually be her third book, name undetermined...

Printed in the United States
By Bookmasters